A
Prosperity
Love Story

A Prosperity Love Story

Rags to Enrichment

A Memoir by
Catherine Ponder

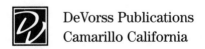

DeVorss Publications
Camarillo California

A Prosperity Love Story
Copyright © 2003
by Catherine Ponder

First Edition, 2003
ISBN: 087516787X
Library of Congress Control Number: 2003101616

Edited by John Niendorff

DeVorss & Company, Publisher
P.O. Box 1389
Camarillo, California 93011-1389
w w w . d e v o r s s . c o m

Printed in Canada

Contents

CHAPTER 4

A New Era Heats Up ~ 33

Happy observations; The fringe benefits; Surprisingly, a writing career begins; Unexpected events; The plot thickens; Further developments; Definite guidance; Facing the music; Love of the deep South.

CHAPTER 5

The Stars Begin To Fall On Alabama ~ 45

Across a crowded room; Unforeseen changes; A spiritual mentor; Unexpected results; Deep South feelings asserted; To the rescue; An additional mantle; Objections overruled; Bound for the great Southwest.

CHAPTER 6

The Stars That Fell On Alabama Landed ~ 55

The secret of pulling things together; Meeting the next deadline; Richard's early days in Birmingham; Richard's investigative abilities; His financial investigative abilities; Richard's other financial activities; Richard's sports activities; A special visit; An analysis of this era.

CHAPTER 7

A Launching Pad Into The Future ~ 67

My financial request; A premonition?; From recession to abundance; From recession to wholeness; The businessmen who helped me; Staff results; Our go-cart Christmas; A cosmic correspondence; A cosmic consciousness experience; A cosmic invitation.

CHAPTER 8

The Heart-Of-Texas Saga Begins ~ 81

The majestic setting; Wonders never cease; Houston; Austin; Florida; Launching a new life; Testings and rewards; A brazen request; Our local setting; An unexpected event; Now what?; Bitter and sweet; In tribute; A memorable anniversary gift.

CHAPTER 9

That Special Saga Continues ~ 99

A new life develops; Coming home; Fiesta time begins for me; Fiesta time continues; Tonic time; No place like home; An unexpected encounter; Reappearance of an old feeling.

CHAPTER 10

Hollywood On The Desert ~ 113

The countess; How a prediction came true; Life—Palm Springs style; Entertaining—Palm Springs style; Going global; Work and play; The Stetson; There goes the neighborhood; Hollywood neighbors—past and present; Celebrity sightings; Normal at last.

CHAPTER 11

The Palm Springs Saga Continues ~ 131

Connecting with the City of Angels; Who would have believed it?; Mother; My beautification program; Celebration time; My estate workplace; The propaganda that backfired; A traumatic change; A godsend; How to get through transitional times.

Acknowledgments

I would like to thank and acknowledge John Niendorff, for his work in editing this manuscript, and a world wide readership, whose encouragement, appreciation, generosity, and financial support have cheered on the author and made her life easier and her work far more successful during the twentieth century and continuing into the twenty-first century.

Special thanks to all from a grateful heart.

— *Catherine Ponder*

SPECIAL NOTE

This book is a series of informal, personal reflections of the author's life. It makes no attempt to be an exhaustive or detailed narrative. As in her other writings, names, places, and dates are not necessarily given. Instead, she prefers to emphasize the overall impact of her life story.

Introduction

RAGS TO ENRICHMENT

Mine has been described by some as a rags-to-riches story. (A great rumor!) I prefer to think of it as a "rags-to-enrichment experience"—one that has spanned a lifetime.

"Age," as the saying goes, "doesn't matter unless you are a fine wine." So now that I am in the "fine wine" category, it seems appropriate for me to share with a worldwide readership what I have learned through the good times as well as the difficult times in my always eventful and sometimes even colorful life.

Upon reflection, I realize that the entirety of my experience has actually been a love story in varied proportions—on some occasions overtly romantic and on others an encounter with the deeper, more subtle initiations of love. Yet everything that's happened has been part of the overall fabric of this thing called life.

I trust that some of the love-lessons I have learned will inspire and benefit you. So here's to our mutual and ever-expanding "enrichment." And here's to the power of love—in its many-faceted forms!

— *Catherine Ponder*

A
Prosperity
Love Story

CHAPTER 1

Catherine's Wartime Washington

"Life is what happens when you're making other plans." I had made other plans. And then life happened.

During World War II, my youthful ambitions were, in fact, turned upside down, as were those of so many others of all ages. My plans had been to work my way through college, after which I would do something I'd felt strongly all my life was to be "special and different"—though I didn't know exactly what it would be. My family assumed that after college I would become an old-maid schoolteacher, since I was more interested in books than boys. At least, they were right about what really interested me, and I gladly left the latter to my party-loving sister.

I did have a beau but did not take him seriously. He regularly began his contemplations of the future by saying, "After the war, when we get married . . ." My reply was always the same, "I won't have time to marry you or anyone else. I have to go off and try to become rich and famous."

He found that statement not only outrageous but hugely amusing as well, since I was very much the product of simpler, prewar times in a quiet corner of the southeastern United States. I still wore homemade dresses and owned only one pair of good, store-bought shoes. Hardly a candidate for rich-and-famous.

However, from the time I was a tiny girl, I'd had the feeling that I was supposed to do something special and different in life, and I easily imagined "rich and famous" would be part of it. Little did I realize how *completely* different my life was to be—beginning with World War II.

THE CAREFREE LIFE OF A GOVERNMENT GIRL

At the last minute, life happened and my plans changed. I decided to delay college in order to go to wartime Washington, D.C., as what was called "a Government Girl." My parents would not have allowed me to do so had it not been that I'd be working for the Federal Bureau of Investigation, one of the most revered government agencies of that era. Also, my family was assured that I would live and work in a protected environment, with almost every action chaperoned or monitored.

Monitored or not, it was an electric atmosphere for an unsophisticated young girl to be thrust into. One prominent socialite described wartime Washington as "the most exciting city in the world." I would hardly have disagreed.

We Government Girls were recruited for all branches of the government to relieve and replace male employees, freeing them for military duty, usually in either the European or Pacific theater of war. We were considered an important part of the war effort, and Uncle Sam went to great lengths to make us happy. The government felt it had to keep its temporary help in wartime Washington well-entertained, so they would not become homesick and leave their jobs before the war was over, even though some did. Therefore, from a social standpoint, my life seemed suddenly to become considerably more stimulating, even festive.

I lived in one of the Government Girls' dormitories at West Potomac Park, on the banks of the Potomac

River near the Lincoln Memorial. In the spring of the year, the famed cherry blossoms abruptly appeared nearby, a glorious sight. The Tidal Basin was in the background, and the recently completed Jefferson Memorial was visible down the Potomac. A much larger complex of Government Girls' dormitories known as "Arlington Farms" was located across the river, in Virginia.

THE SOCIAL LIFE OF A GOVERNMENT GIRL

I paid $26 a month for a room the size of a walk-in closet. It had one window and a small area for storing luggage and hanging clothing. It was furnished with a tiny single bed, a chair, a table, and a lamp. Restrooms, showers, and laundry facilities were located nearby, in a common area. At the end of the hallway outside was the one telephone, on which all the girls in that wing received calls. Forget privacy. If they wanted to make outgoing calls, they had to find a payphone elsewhere.

Although a number of girls lived in that dorm, I only had time to get acquainted with those in my own wing. They worked for various branches of the government: the Army, Navy, and Selective Service, among others. Some were Southern like me, some were from the Midwest or even the West Coast, and others were those I regarded as "Yankees"—but all were pleasant to be around and some of us even became fast friends for the duration.

I tried to follow their example and get excited about the social life the government had planned for us. We had been provided a Recreation Hall next to our two dorms. There, the military bused in GIs from the many camps in nearby Maryland and Virginia.

Saturday night dances were big events, as were parties at the USO. Sometimes those of us in the dorms were bused to various nearby military bases for parties and dances with the GIs, which were also considered special times. These events were all conducted under close supervision, which—given the general wartime anxiety, uncertainty, and tendency to act spontaneously—was probably not a bad idea.

Obediently, I tried it all, but easily got bored with those comings and goings. I decided that I could find other ways to participate in the social side of the war effort. I realized that my personal style was to socialize through one-on-one contacts with individuals more than it was to join groups for parties, dances, and similar activities. I remember meeting one young soldier who made a particular impression on me. He was from the Midwest, with the manners, class, and style of a Southern gentleman. On his last visit to the dorm to see me, he said he was headed overseas and would write. But he did not, and I later learned he had been killed in one of the major battles of the war only a month after his departure.

That was my sad introduction to having become, very innocently and if only on the home front, part of what would later be called "the greatest generation"—whom Tom Brokaw, author of the famous book of the same name, described as being American citizens who came of age during the Great Depression and World War II and went on to build modern America.

DORM LIFE'S UNIQUE SECURITY SYSTEM

Our activities were watched over by the Dorm Supervisor, who was a former college dean. The rule was that we had to check in by 10 P.M. during the week.

On weekends, check-in time was no later than midnight, when the front door was locked, and we had to sign in the time of our arrival at the front desk. Any girl coming in after 2 A.M. could only gain entrance by contacting the night watchman. More than one or two such late arrivals could lead to a girl's being immediately dismissed from her job, and perhaps being sent home. During my dorm years, though, I never heard of a girl being dismissed. Nor did I hear of anyone becoming pregnant or otherwise getting in real trouble. Indeed, those were kinder, gentler, more innocent times on the home front. For instance, profanity, obscenities, naughty jokes, and off-color stories simply did not exist, at least where we were.

Such were the benefits of security in the dorms, and I preferred it. The many Government Girls who lived in homes with private families may have had different experiences and perspectives, but I preferred the security of dorm life.

Our greatest grief was that of family, friends, or sweethearts getting killed overseas, or being reported as missing in action.

We were allowed to entertain guests in one large public room near the entrance on the main floor. Tables, chairs, and sofas were scattered around its interior, while doorless booths along the walls created a space where several people could carry on a conversation in relative privacy. Almost no one had any excess money for entertainment, so that public room was a convenient place for us to visit. A snack bar was located off the lobby.

Weekends were especially busy times, since family, friends, and boys from home—now in the military and passing through—would often congregate there. Usually the GIs from home brought along other military personnel, so we would invite some of our friends, other Government Girls, to socialize with them there.

This arrangement suited our Dorm Supervisor, since it meant that from her check-in desk at the main doorway, she could watch all of us at one time. No signs of affection, not even hand-holding, were allowed. We were convinced that she had eyes in the back of her head, the presence of which she demonstrated when anyone, at least in her opinion, got a little too friendly.

Perhaps the mainstay of our stability in our wing of the dorm was a lady named Louise, who had worked for the government since World War I. She soothed any concerns we had, loaned us money between paydays, and generally kept us out of each other's hair. Though we all adored her, our darkly humorous observation about her was that she'd stayed with the government so long because she was still waiting for her fiancé to return from World War I. This was actually cruel humor, since we were all aware that he had been killed in France during that previous war. In many ways she made life easier for us; in other ways we kept her occupied and entertained.

THIS GOVERNMENT GIRL'S WORK WEEK

Mondays through Fridays, I was up, dressed, and at the bus stop overlooking the Potomac River by 6:30 A.M. There I caught a bus into downtown Washington, where I boarded a trolley that took me to southeast Washington, where I got on another bus that took me to the National Guard Armory. That building was occupied by the FBI during the war, mainly as a repository for its vast archives of fingerprints records.

As a fingerprint classifier, I sat in a straight-back chair at a small table and looked through a magnifying glass at fingerprints.[1] Rows of identical tables, where other classifiers worked, ran the length of the room, from front to rear, with four to six such rows in each room. A supervisor sat facing us and collected our fingerprint cards each hour, checked them for errors, and recorded the data, along with how many we had finished in that hour.

We were taught a special code for classifying them. It was nerve-wracking, exacting work, but it developed the discipline, concentration, and consistent work ethic that I—and probably many other of the girls—would need for the rest of our lives, though I did not know it then. The tedium of our job was softened now and then by unexpected events, such as our being driven one day to the famed Quantico, Virginia, training center of the FBI, and being given a tour of the FBI building on Pennsylvania Avenue. There we met, then shook hands and chatted with, the well-known J. Edgar Hoover. As a further reward, we were given his personally autographed picture.

My work days at the FBI were enhanced by all the love songs of World War II being played throughout the Armory prior to the beginning of the day, then again at the end of the day. Our immersion in the popular songs of that era, such as "Sentimental Journey" or "I'll Be Seeing You," added to the romantic atmosphere of the times.

During the work week, we were allowed a half-hour break for lunch in the FBI cafeteria, which was my one hot meal of the day. My sustenance the rest of the work week came from the snack bar at the dorm.

---

1. Only in recent times has the complex method of fingerprint classifying been computerized.

On weekends, though, we sometimes went out in groups and dined in greater style. I recall eating at a charming little Italian restaurant located near the illustrious Willard Hotel. I always looked forward to my five-course meal there for $1.50—a real treat. At other times, we went to the popular Hot Shoppes or to the casual White Castle hamburger sit-at-the-counter restaurants that were located around the city. In general, where we ate was likely to be determined by the calendar—meaning when our next paycheck was due.

THE CULTURAL REWARDS

About the time I realized that being part of the usual wartime social scene of Washington was not necessarily my patriotic duty, I met a much-needed new friend.

She, too, worked for the FBI, and she informed me that she also was not interested in the dances and parties provided for us by the government. She was very focused and goal-oriented, and thus a good influence on me at the time. She had already planned exactly how long she intended to work in Washington and how much money she intended to save, after which she was going to return home and work her way through college. She was very proud that her father was on the staff of the Green Bay Packers in Wisconsin.

When she suggested that I accompany her to various of the city's cultural sites and events, I was elated. So we began spending our weekends visiting various museums. Among the most impressive to me was the National Gallery of Art, commonly called "the Mellon Art Gallery" in honor of its founder. We enjoyed its featured piano, violin, and harp concerts in a beautiful garden setting. We also visited the famed Smithsonian Institute, the Washington Cathedral, and other similar places that opened a new world to me. We attended performances by the National Symphony Orchestra and visited Constitution Hall, where we heard the piano artistry and unusual wit of Oscar Levant. After a performance at the National Theater, we waited back-stage to greet Diana Barrymore.

We were unable to tour the White House or the Washington Monument, which were closed to visitors for the duration of the war.

We sometimes attended Loew's Capitol Theater, where we were entertained by wartime movies filled with the patriotic sentiments of the times. These were followed by hour-long stage shows featuring various entertainers from the Big Band era: Vaughn Monroe, Woody Herman, the Ink Spots, the Mills Brothers, Charlie Spivak, Spike Jones and the City Slickers, Guy Lombardo, Charlie Barnett, Gene Krupa, and others— now all legends.

Vaudeville acts and variety shows were often part of the program. Beautiful Lana Turner, Ginny Simms, and other stars appeared, on their way to or from entertaining the troops. That period was my introduction to a life-long love of the theater and the arts in general.

One example of what passed for humor in those days was this, the most famous vaudeville joke of the era, which was oft-repeated:

Woman #1: I sent my husband out for a loaf of bread twenty years ago, and he never returned.

Woman #2: What's the problem?

Woman #1: Should I go out and get that loaf of bread myself, or should I keep waiting for him to come back?

Another well-known example of wartime humor came from Great Britain, with this description of what bothered the British about U.S. troops: "The American GI is overpaid, overfed, oversexed—and over here."

It was believed that such silliness helped relieve the tension of the war effort.

Other memorable events occurred. For instance, during that time President Roosevelt ordered home the three surviving members of the group that raised the American flag on the tiny island of Iwo Jima after one of the bloodiest battles in the South Pacific. In their cross-country tour to sell war bonds, they were hailed as heroes, and I saw them at the Capitol Theater. All of the men involved in that flag-raising were Marines except one, a Navy hospital corpsman who later received the Navy Cross for his bravery. Among them, he lived the longest—until 1994.

A PLEASANT SURPRISE

At regular intervals, we fingerprint classifiers were evaluated for our accuracy and speed. The results could mean dismissal or promotion. Since I tended to be a slow classifier, I was concerned about my evaluation. My fellow workers assumed I would flunk out. I tended to agree with them.

Wondering what to do, I suddenly remembered that whenever my parents were facing difficulty, my father always said to my mother, "Write those people out there in Missouri—you know, Silent Unity—and tell them to straighten out this problem." My little mother would dutifully write the famous nondenominational Prayer Department of the Unity School of Christianity in Unity Village, Missouri, and, indeed, the problem would get "straightened out."

I decided I had nothing to lose by trying the same method. When I wrote Silent Unity asking for prayers, they graciously replied, which was enormously reassuring. And when the results of the evaluations were revealed, I not only didn't flunk out, but I was also one of two people in our entire section to receive a promotion and a raise—from $1440 a year to $1620. My colleagues viewed me with suspicion at first, for they had assumed what I had assumed: that I'd never make it and would probably wash out. Their suspicion was followed at first by total dismay, but ultimately by vast respect.

I did not know enough in those days to write Silent Unity and thank them for helping me. Even if I had done so, I would not have included an appropriate "thank you" offering. I just didn't know any better.

Nevertheless, an inner light came on as a result of that experience, and I started to realize that forces well beyond my everyday comprehension were available to me when I needed help. Thus began my lifelong involvement with those deeper powers and my search to understand how they could be used to promote and enhance other people's well-being as well as my own. What it also meant was that I had just been introduced, if only briefly, to what would become the overall love of my life, the full importance of which was to surface only with the passing of time.

CHAPTER 2

When The Boys Came Home

In the midst of early-morning work weeks and varied social weekends, most of us in my dorm were also busy with another wartime activity: writing to everybody we knew. So many lonely, homesick young men were stationed at military installations, both in this country and all across the world. Some were relatives, others friends. And then there were sweethearts—the boys most of the girls hoped to marry when the war was over.

Until I got into the romantic atmosphere of wartime Washington, I was perfectly happy not to be among that starry-eyed group. Marriage was not something I had regarded as a viable option for myself, as I still maintained the private notion that there was something "special and different" I was supposed to do in life.

LOVE AT FIRST SIGHT

Nevertheless, I had been smitten since the age of fourteen. It happened when my father was visited at our house by a relative, a man who had married into my father's family. This man brought along his son Joe, and for me it was love at first sight. I could not explain how I knew this was "it," but I deeply felt that way. Joe was a year older than I was, and though we barely said more than a few words to each other, on some mysterious "other" level I felt I had met my match.

When I visited an out-of-town cousin during the next couple of summers at my great aunt's house, this young man came by often, since he spent the summer months with his father nearby. I was quietly fascinated with him, and bells rang in my teenage heart. I thought I could even see a curious kind of glow around him. "So this is how it works," I mused.

As I continued quietly observing Joe, I said nothing to anyone. But by the time I was sweet sixteen, I was privately in love, though I wasn't sure how those feelings were going to fit into my "special and different" life-schedule. Still, when I compared him to the local boys who were available for dating, they just didn't measure up.

Unfortunately, however, it was all a fantasy. Joe lived out of town and had, so far as I was aware, never even noticed me. My fantasy might have seemed preposterous if anyone had known about it. But no one did, and I was prepared to play a waiting game.

HOW IT ALL BEGAN

When I got to Washington the following year, I began to think about Joe strongly.

Most of the others in my wing of the dorm had beaus overseas: predominately in the Army and Navy. So lots of government-censored letters from various theaters of war in Europe and the Pacific were shared among my dorm-mates. After considering for a long time whether I should try to contact him, I finally, bravely, wrote Joe at the last address I had for him. But weeks went by and, having heard nothing, I dismissed it as a great try that didn't work out.

Then one evening after a tedious day of classifying fingerprints, followed by a long ride home via trolley and bus, I found a letter in my box at the dorm. I didn't recognize the handwriting on the envelope, nor did

I understand the complicated return address, that of a military installation I'd never heard of on the West Coast. But when I looked more closely at the name on the return address, my puzzlement was replaced by sudden joy. I was elated! My "great try" *had* caught on!

Joe wrote that he remembered me and was glad to have mail from wartime Washington, which all seemed very glamorous to him.

I was overwhelmed but delighted to finally have his attention—and at a time when that kind of communication was exactly what we both needed most. This sailor and the shy Government Girl were on their way to a wartime romance by mail. I doubt that it could have happened any other way.

That Joe and I seemed destined to make contact was revealed by the way he got that first letter from me. For the sake of personal privacy, I had deliberately not tried to reach him directly, through either his father or my father's relatives. I did not want my interest in him or his possible non-reaction to be subject to family scrutiny or to become a source of gossip. But fate finally dealt me what I considered to be a friendly hand.

He and his mother (who was divorced from his father) had moved from the address to which I sent that first letter. But the mailman, being a helpful neighbor, left my letter with the nearby cleaners that he knew Joe's mother frequented. When she picked up the letter there, she was impressed that it was from Washington, D.C., so she sent it on to her son, just before he shipped out for duty in the Pacific. And the connection was made.

IN OUR DORM AT THE END OF THE WAR

Years later, the business world was to learn about the power of direct mail. It all became clear enough for me in World War II.

To say that Joe and I looked forward to each other's letters would be putting it mildly. We lived for them. He sent me souvenirs along with his letters when he was in port in Hawaii and later in the South Pacific. I savored and saved them all—the letters, the souvenirs, and the memories of that special era, now lost in the mist of time.

Then came the end of the war: "When Johnnie Came Marching Home." Phase I: Europe. Phase II: the Pacific. The boys from the European theater came home first, because the war there ended a few months before it did in the Pacific and also because more military craft were reportedly available in Europe to bring back the huge numbers of troops. What an exciting, romantic time it was!

Among the beaus of the girls in my dorm wing, we knew the first to return home would be a particular soldier who'd fought in Europe. He had gotten engaged to Sarah, a schoolteacher-turned-Government Girl, prior to going overseas. We had never met him.

All of us in our dorm wing knew when he was scheduled to arrive, so we mischievously set up a surprise for their long-delayed homecoming meeting—which was to take place in the dorm's public lobby. We arranged for the Dorm Supervisor to telephone Sarah upstairs when her GI arrived. When the call came, we all abruptly "got busy" and quickly disappeared—downstairs to the lobby—while Sarah lagged behind to complete getting ready for her meeting. She was so nervous that she hadn't a clue about our strange mass vanishing act.

Most of us Government Girls were in our late teens, but Sarah was an ancient twenty-four, which we felt put her well past her prime. So we were all curious about what kind of soldier she, at her advanced, over-the-hill age, might be engaged to. When he walked in, we gasped! In his military uniform, he was knock-out gorgeous, and a collective sense of awe swept through us—

along with a new respect for what a twenty-four-year-old Government Girl could do.

When nervous Sarah innocently appeared in the lobby, he was waiting, so handsome and happy, with open arms. Both of them were in tears. We were all waiting too—about a dozen deep—with open eyes and ears. Sarah was so thrilled to see her long-awaited love that several minutes went by before she realized she also had an uninvited but enthusiastic cheering section taking it all in.

ONE BRIGHT SHINING MOMENT

I did not take any chances on being the victim of such antics when my own long-awaited sailor came home from the Pacific. As we'd pre-arranged, he telephoned me at the dorm in the middle of the night from San Francisco when his ship finally docked. He then proceeded cross-country for a short visit with his mother, after which he took a bus to Washington.

I arranged to meet him at the bus station at 6 A.M. on a Saturday morning, so we would have the weekend to get re-acquainted in person. Though he was now free to wear civilian clothes and very much wanted to do so, I insisted that for this first visit he allow me to see him in uniform. Since he was anxious to be a civilian again, this was not a suggestion he welcomed, but he graciously complied.

After a joyous reunion at the bus station, we went out to breakfast and talked and talked and talked. I felt as though we had always known each other. Later in the morning, we took a cab back to the dorm, where the girls were charmed with his friendliness and Southern manners. That night we had dinner at what for me was a "fancy restaurant." The resident photographer took a picture of this Government Girl in her bright silk, floral blouse with a black background, smart black wraparound skirt, and high heels. But even with me in those heels, the size-difference between us was remarkable, since he was over six feet tall and I was every bit of 5' 3"—and weighed all of 100 pounds!

What I would give today for that picture, but it has long since disappeared, together with those letters he wrote me during the war.

That weekend after his homecoming and the months that followed stand out as one of those highly emotional, brief-shining-Camelot moments we all yearn to experience. He called every night from his mother's home, where he was staying, a few hours' train ride away from Washington. Most weekends he took the train or bus to visit me, and we had a glorious time getting better acquainted, as we went sightseeing in the nation's capital and enjoyed its many fine restaurants, art galleries, museums, and musical concerts. It must have been love, since I even consented to let him "Take Me Out to the Ball Game," though I was not the greatest of sports fans. During that period, we developed much happiness and congeniality, as well as many expectations for a happy future together.

Then over lunch at a Chinese restaurant one Saturday, he just happened to recall his military stint in California, before he went to the Pacific. He told me how much he loved California and how he would like to return there to live and work someday. He spoke of many servicemen having played golf with Bob Hope and Bing Crosby, something the two entertainers reportedly did during the war.

Innocently I said, meaning it as light-hearted banter, "When you go to California to live, give me a ring"—I meant a *telephone* ring—"and maybe I'll join you."

Rather seriously, he replied, "I've been thinking about that."

"What?" I asked. "Going to California?"

"No," he replied quietly. "Giving you a ring."

Even though I was surprised by this sudden turn of events, that conversation became the verbal beginning to an engagement.

FURTHER GET-ACQUAINTED TIMES

A month or so later, I went by train to his hometown on a weekend to meet his mother. I wore a gray gabardine suit with a borrowed gold blouse and those high heels. We all had a happy time together.

His mother was, I realized much later, a unique woman, far ahead of her time. A decade or so earlier, in the 1930s, she reportedly endured an abusive marriage—for as long as she could take it. Even though divorcing her husband made her a social outcast during that era, she dared to do it. And so, with Joe, his younger sister, and an elderly mother to provide for, this emotionally scarred and scared lady went to work and brought in a humble income that helped them all survive. (She was supposed to get a court-ordered $15-per-month child support payment, but collecting it from a man who was unwilling to pay it proved too much of a burden to pursue.)

By the time I met Joe's mother, *her* mother had died of natural causes and her daughter, Joe's sister, had died as a result of an accident. So she seemed to welcome me as pleasant, caring, feminine company. I also welcomed her into my life, and I was fascinated to observe how different her actions were from what passed in those days as conventional behavior. She smoked openly, had a cocktail now and then, and sometimes even dated men from the nearby military base, where she'd worked during the war. I was delighted with her bright mind, quick wit, and friendly, talkative manner. Her son had obviously inherited her fun-loving personality.

A FAST PACE OF COME AND GO

After that long weekend visit, things moved at a fast pace. The three of us soon took a trip to my parents' home out of state in order for the two families to meet and for Joe and me to talk to them about our engagement.

However, what I did not count on was my no-nonsense parents. My devout, churchgoing mother did not know how to take this witty, divorced, chain-smoking woman who worked for a living instead of being a home-maker. While my father rejoiced that his eldest child would soon be married and out of the house forever, my mother and Joe's mother continued trying to make their adjustments to each other. It never happened.

As the weeks went by after Joe and I returned to our respective homes, we exchanged letters, phone calls, and visits, and soon realized that a traditional wedding was out of the question. It would have involved far too many details, too many people who needed to be pleased, and too much money. The only solution was—in terms of the language of that day—to "run off and get married." So we did, and we never regretted it. But our actions were a bitter disappointment to both our mothers—each for different reasons, as I learned later.

When Joe and I discovered during our first year of marriage that we were going to have a baby, my mother was elated, because it would be her first grandchild. Joe's mother, however, felt he was too young to take on the responsibility of both a wife and a baby. She also felt her son should not be distracted from the college education she had long dreamed he would get. She did not see how we could work it out—how we could have a baby and he could still get a good education. Aside from those specifics, she was concerned in general that this "country girl with no money and no social connections" would hold her son down to the level of mediocrity she, herself, had personally endured for so long. To all appearances she was right.

Faced with his mother's strong opinion that I would never amount to anything and might even hinder his progress, Joe was caught in a no-win situation, torn between love for his long-suffering, hard-working mother (and all she reminded him she had done for him) and his young wife and baby. Just a little emotional support from either side of the family for our marriage could have helped us make it. But we didn't have that support then, nor did we have it later.

SURPRISE TIME

As suddenly as our brief marriage had begun, just that suddenly did Joe and I separate— temporarily we thought. We did it in part hoping to keep down friction between his family and mine. Also, my fun-loving husband was not sure, once he experienced it, that he was ready for the responsibilities of a family. He decided his mother might be right, but he wanted to make that determination for himself. I also wanted time to think things through.

So we decided to give each other time to re-examine our situation and to determine our futures—whether they would be together or separate. Although I was personally devastated by this turn of events, I did not wear my broken heart on my sleeve. This was what childhood training in my non-emotional family had taught me.

Stunned, even numb, though I was, I decided to bide my time quietly. Not even my family—my parents, sister, and brother—knew how wounded I felt emotionally.

My father tried to explain it all away as "a wartime marriage." Hardly. It was much more than that. "They were too young." Nonsense. The heart knows no age.

A BIGGER LOVE STORY BEGINS

Now, more than fifty years afterward, I still can feel the painful disappointment of those times, not to mention all the emotional, physical, and financial suffering they were to cause my son and me. And yet that saying— "There's no love like your first love"—still rings true.

Wise people have said we all come into this world for two purposes: to learn and to teach. If that's so, what did I learn from this heart-wrenching experience, and what was I then able to teach?

First, I learned that having a pleasant, fun-loving husband is not always fun. *Second*, I learned that negative attitudes in others—in my case, my mother-in-law's disapproval—can be powerful, if hard-to-take, incentives to succeed. Her disapproval was what I needed to help me start developing my own abilities and begin making something of myself. That has proved to be a lifetime project. *Third*, during that era, seeds were planted for the development of the motto I have shared with countless people ever since: "No matter what happens, hold up your head and keep going—and growing." And its companion: "Our lives are shaped by those who love us and by those who refuse to love us."

Regardless, my greatest reward from that period was twofold. It gave me my only child, who in various ways would ultimately help me survive a lifetime of both challenges and blessings. And it led me to a slow realization that the "something special and different" feeling I had felt since childhood was coming back—strong.

CHAPTER 3

A New Era Begins

When I brought Richard home, my mother—his "Granny"—was delighted to take charge of her first grandchild. She was destined to become his most enthusiastic cheerleader, and he, in return, would regard her as the great love of his life.

My father very graciously loaned me enough money that I could work my way through business college. After I graduated, that business college helped me find a full-time job as a legal secretary.

Why didn't I insist on financial support from my husband, especially for my son? Such was my independent nature that I did not care to be beholden to anyone, even my own husband. Furthermore, my proud Southern family would not hear of it and strongly supported my decision to be independent of him. If he'd had the means and voluntarily shared his resources with my son and me, that would have been fine. But he didn't. He was involved with his own life—with his own present and future—as was I with mine, so it became and remained a moot question between us. His lack of financial or emotional support later turned out to be a blessing in disguise.

A NEW JOB, A NEW WAY OF LIFE

The man I worked for at my new job was a Phi Beta Kappa attorney educated at Duke and Harvard. He had gone into practice with his father, a well-known title lawyer, in the old Knights of Columbus Building, located at the Market Square only a few miles from my family home. His father and his father's longtime secretary occupied one office, while my boss and I occupied a second office. Both offices were filled with interesting old antique furniture. Valuable it may have been; comfortable it was not.

The heat was inadequate and air conditioning was unavailable. On cold days, we kept extra sweaters and jackets on hand and hovered around an ancient potbellied stove. On hot days we opened wide the windows. When clients appeared in these quarters, each of us secretaries, for the sake of their confidentiality, went out into the large Knights of Columbus hall and sat on the steps leading downstairs, until our bosses' client-conferences were completed.

Later we moved into a brand-new air-conditioned bank building, with all new furniture, where we occupied the second floor. My boss's father continued his work as a title lawyer and also functioned as vice-president of that bank.

Meanwhile, my boss was busy building up a general practice and becoming a corporate attorney. He handled most of the legal work for the early shopping centers and condos that were developing during the postwar building boom in our area.

When he was elected mayor of our town, his law office also became "Office of the Mayor," since the City Hall had no room for it. This meant I had to meet, become socially conversant with, and act as hostess to all types of "visiting firemen." My job thus proved to be a training ground where, altogether unexpectedly but to my great benefit, I developed both my social and mental skills, on paper and in person.

My boss was also working his way up the ladder in community service: Kiwanis International and teaching a Sunday School class were two of his pet projects. I had quite a time trying to keep up with his business and social activities as well as with his strong work ethic. Neither of us had even a glimmer of why I was being indoctrinated in so many aspects and areas of work. Or that any of it might be related to the something "special and different" that still lay ahead for me.

THE GREATEST DISCOVERY OF MY LIFE

When I became active in a prominent local Protestant church, my popularity there was doubtless due to my title as "Secretary to the Mayor." Rightly or wrongly, some townspeople felt that if they couldn't influence the mayor, the next best thing was to make an impression on his secretary. I enjoyed basking in his reflected glory, but I recognized its basis and did not take it seriously.

During those action-packed years, I did a casual thing one day that was destined eventually to turn my life upside down—again. My mother had long been a reader of nondenominational literature, though she said nothing about it to either my father or me. Instead, she constantly placed it all over our house in the hope that my father would pick it up and get interested. She thought he "needed" it. He never took the hint.

One day I got so tired of moving her literature out of my way that I idly opened a piece of it to determine what kind of propaganda my mother was trying to push off on my father.

When I began to read about the mind being the connecting link between a God of love and humankind, and that I was a spiritual being who was having a human experience that was giving me a chance to grow, learn, and expand my world—I was astonished. What a shock! The ideas I found there were what I had vaguely believed ever since I was a child. What they showed me now, clearly and directly, was the outlook I needed to get on with my life. Why had my mother never told me what was in those little booklets?

I went quietly to her bookshelf and found a thin little volume titled *Lessons in Truth.*[2] It was written by H. Emilie Cady, who, at the turn of the twentieth century, was reported to have been the first lady doctor in New York City. The opening chapter caught my attention. It was called "Bondage or Liberty, Which?" A good question, I thought. Then I read:

> No person or thing in the universe, no chain of circumstances, can by any possibility interpose itself between you and all good. You may think that something stands between you and your heart's desire, and so live with that desire unfulfilled; but it is not true. Deny it and you will see clearly that nothing can stand between you and your good.

Wow!

INTRODUCTION TO THE PROSPERITY TEACHING

From a prosperity standpoint, I learned *first* what I needed to learn *most*. When I looked at the book list, I found just one book listed as free. I ordered it, since it was about all I could manage at the time anyway. It was

---

2. *Lessons in Truth*, by H. Emilie Cady (Unity School of Christianity, Unity Village, MO 64065).

entitled *As You Tithe, So You Prosper*[3]—and the word "prosper" is what caught my eye.

When the book arrived in the mail, I read it right through and realized that its ideas made complete and total sense. I immediately began tithing ten percent off the top of my weekly income of $25—a grand total of $2.50.

I learned later of a man who went from rags to riches through tithing, who said, "I would be in the poorhouse if I did not put God first financially. Sharing is the beginning of financial increase." His giving made him rich. The people of the East believe sharing is the first step to enlightenment and enrichment, because it opens you up inwardly—as well as outwardly—to receive. In fact, my parents had tithed sporadically and often commented on how much better things went when they tithed. However, they somehow never got the message that doing so *regularly* would cause them to reap benefits regularly.

Now, after a fifty-year period of regular tithing, I can attest to its prospering power, gradual though it may have been for me. The simple act of putting God first financially seems to supercede and encompass all the other prosperity laws, even as important as they are individually.

SCARS CAN LEAD TO STARS

With my Southern heritage, I had been taught to believe that "a Southern lady" had one basic role to play in life. It had three parts: get married, have children, and mind her husband.

---

3. *As You Tithe, So You Prosper,* by L. E. Meyer (Unity School of Christianity, Unity Village, MO 64065).

If, in addition to those accepted roles, she needed to work for a living, three options were usually available: to become a nurse, a teacher, or a secretary—but only for a certain period to meet a specific family need. Once that need was met, her job returned to being a homemaker and acting as hostess for her husband and family. But life was not to be that clear-cut for me.

The status of my marriage was still being determined when I was informed of the sudden demise of my husband. My father confirmed it through his family connections. Sometime much later, my mother-in-law also passed on. Though both of them were gone now, what they had contributed to my life was destined to help lead me from "scars to stars" in my growth and progress over the coming years.

LOSING LEADS TO WINNING

With the matter of my husband now permanently settled, I privately took up a serious study of all the inspirational literature and books I could get—with specific attention on matters of my personal well-being. I asked myself, "Is this all there is—working day in and out, plus many evenings and weekends, but still able to provide only the bare necessities for myself and my son?" I had a haunting feeling it was not. (My tithing hadn't yet had a chance to show forth its benefits, which were to be reflected in many ways later.)

Thus for two years I prayed for a home for myself and my son. Yet the only answer I received was a familiar Biblical one: "But seek ye first the kingdom of God, and His righteousness; and all these things shall be added unto you." (Matthew 6:33) In response, I thought, "Oh no, dear God, there must be an easier way than *that*!"

Then an unexpected thing happened that was to be the beginning of a major change in my life. My boss decided to run for Congress. In addition to his general and corporate practice of law, his ever-expanding community work, and his serving two terms as Mayor—now this! I wondered how could I possibly take on the added work and responsibility his new decision implied. Yet I knew I must try.

Months later, when his nonstop campaign was over, he had lost by only a few thousand votes. I was exhausted. So I bravely went into his office and said, "Boss, I'm sorry you lost, but I am so tired that I must have some time off."

"How much time are you thinking about?" he asked.

I knew he figured I might want to take about two weeks.

"Six weeks," I said.

"*Six* weeks? Catherine, you know there's no way you can take off six weeks. How can I practice law without a secretary for that long? And what do you need six weeks off for?"

"I want to go to Unity Village, in Missouri, and take some courses in 'self-improvement.' "

He agreed that I needed all the self-improvement I could get and reluctantly said I could take the time.

Later I realized that although he had lost the Congressional campaign, I had won. Because that six weeks at Unity Village was divinely ordained to change my life forever.

A STEP TOWARD FULFILLMENT

When I asked my mother to look after young Richard for a month and a half while I took a bus trip to Kansas City, she replied, "Why don't you get your inspiration at your own church? Why do you have to go halfway across the United States for it?"

I told her I'd already tried that, and it helped. "I met lots of nice people and I loved the minister. But I don't just need regular Christianity. I need 'practical' Christianity. That's what these people offer in their literature. I want to check them out in person." I told her it all sounded too good to be true.

My father walked the floor, wringing his hands over my boarding a bus and traveling two days and two nights alone to a place I had never seen and knew nothing much about. But I, nevertheless, was on my way— in more ways than any of us dreamed possible. The feeling that had haunted me since childhood that I was going to do something "special and different" was about to take its first step toward fulfillment.

RICHARD AND HIS "GRANNY"

In the midst of all my varied experiences, what was my son up to?

From the start, Richard always had a mind of his own. Since he was his Granny's first grandchild, he could do no wrong. He thought he ruled her with an iron fist emotionally, and his ever-wise grandmother, knowing his personality, let him think he was doing so. "Diplomacy," she observed, "is the ability to let someone else do it your way."

She tried to help him "get religion" by taking him with her to church functions, which were endless: prayer meetings, women's church meetings (where he was the only male present), and Sunday school and church services each week. He kept trying to think of ways to skip them all, but never quite got it figured out.

He loved working in the flower and vegetable gardens his Granny constantly tended at home. Doing so afforded him an opportunity to give her lots of advice about how to plant flowers and vegetables, and she appeared to listen. Sometimes the flowers lived and sometimes they did not, but his Granny still listened. When a friend commented on her unique gardening methods, she said, "Look, I am raising more than just flowers and vegetables here." End of subject.

RICHARD'S EARLY ADVENTURES

When Richard was four years old, I talked the kindergarten director of my church into enrolling him there a year earlier than ordinarily would have been permitted (this was before preschools for even earlier ages were the norm). I felt he needed to become adapted to children his own age, since he had only adults at home—his grandparents and me—from whom he might learn how to get along with other people.

The first day, when I picked him up at noon, the director said, "Your son doesn't know how to relate to other children, so he got a black eye."

I said, "That's the reason he's here—to learn how to relate to other children."

We didn't need to have *that* discussion again!

For two years, Richard boarded a city bus with me each workday and rode into town. There I walked with him over to the church kindergarten on my way to my office, some blocks away. Then I rushed back at noon, in time to put him on the city bus by himself, homeward bound.

Many of his fellow bus riders considered this unusual: a four-year-old traveling home alone. But he quickly made friends with people of all ages. And mysteriously, he began to have pocket change, which neither his

Granny nor I had given him. Apparently, others on those bus trips marveled at his ability and poise while traveling alone at such an early age and rewarded him accordingly. Furthermore, he never got another black eye in kindergarten.

DIFFERENT DRUMMERS

And so had begun mine and Richard's sagas—separate yet together—that would lead continually to our both engaging life in its many facets and phases, in diverse parts of the country, in various lines of work, and in various experiences of relationship, romance, and marriage, as each of us—mother and son—listened to our own different drummers.

CHAPTER 4

A New Era Heats Up

What a surprise Unity School turned out to be! Located in Unity Village, Missouri, it had sprawling grounds, red-tile-roofed buildings, an abundance of colorful flowerbeds, and beautiful shrubbery everywhere else; it also had inviting nooks and crannies where one could sit quietly to read, study, meditate, or just soak up the peaceful atmosphere, as birds, butterflies, and an occasional rabbit passed by. It was hardly the primitive "camp down by the river" environment I had assumed I would have to endure.

And that was not my only surprise. When I first arrived, ready for some solitude and a good night's sleep following those two days and nights on buses, I discovered I would have a roommate. As the station wagon delivered me and my luggage to the nearby cottage where I would be staying, a young woman emerged and said enthusiastically, "Where have you been? I've been waiting for you."

What a wonderful introduction! What a welcome!

HAPPY OBSERVATIONS

Unity School turned out to be everything I could have hoped for and, at the same time, it was amazingly different. I literally couldn't have been prepared in advance for what it was like, simply because I'd never before encountered, much less imagined that I'd be in, such an atmosphere.

People from all over the world, from every walk of life, were gathered together to study age-old Truths that made us feel we were special and could be winners, no matter what life had thrown at us. The instructors, many of whom were women, looked like gods and goddesses to me. I had never known that people in spiritual work could be so good-looking! None of the women had the usual drab, "run-down-at-the-heels," plain-Jane look I'd often encountered in religious types. These people wore colorful clothes, with appropriate make-up, jewelry, and accessories to match. The men all looked like movie stars to my provincial mind.

Not only did they look good, sound good, and have uplifting messages to share, but they were also very down-to-earth, friendly, and approachable. The president of the school and his brother, also a school official, were often out and around, available for a chat with visitors and students. They presented no "holier-than-thou" attitudes.

When a fellow student came back to our cottage from an early-morning walk, she mentioned what a nice "gardener" she had just met. He had proudly shown her the variety of colorful flowers he was lovingly tending behind a beautiful house on the grounds.

Later, when we attended a morning meditation session for the students, she was startled to discover that her "gardener" was leading the meditation! His day job, as things turned out, was being the president of Unity School! He was Lowell Fillmore, son of the founders.

The vice-president of the school was one of the most attractive, ageless women I'd ever seen. Not only her looks and manner but also the public meditations she led always left me feeling that I had just died and gone to heaven—and was loving it. One of her favorite statements was, "I AM YOUNG, STRONG, AND HEALTHY. MY BODY KNOWS IT AND MY BODY SHOWS IT. "

During my time there, I also had an opportunity to experience my first formal church service—at Unity Temple, on Country Club Plaza in Kansas City. It was considered the "Mother Church of the Unity Movement" and revered as such. Uncharacteristically and with great embarrassment, I cried all the way through the service in the packed house. I thought, "At last, I'm 'home,'" and that Sunday service left me in an indescribable, uplifted state for days. The feeling was not necessarily because of what the speaker, Reverend L. E. Meyer, had said or how he said it. Rather it was a result of the total package—the message, the music, the elegant surroundings, and the feeling of oneness among the congregation.

THE FRINGE BENEFITS

During the following weeks, as I went to classes, met people from around the world, and enjoyed the overall atmosphere of peace and beauty, the inner pressure and tension from my hard-working lifestyle back home began to fade away. For the first time in several years I felt as though I could make it. Only this time I had some spiritual and mental tools to help me. That lifelong feeling of having a "special and different" mission and approach to living was beginning to make a little sense.

In fact, it made so much sense that at the end of my first visit to Unity School, I did not want to leave and return to a demanding job and lifestyle back home. My boss sensed my reluctance, which was not difficult for him, since I had not returned at the end of the six weeks. Assuming the reason was that I had run out of money, he wrote me a nice letter, enclosed an extra week's pay, and asked me please to come home and straighten out the files so he could begin practicing law again. He had obviously discovered that I'd developed my own private file system, better known as "job security."

SURPRISINGLY, A WRITING CAREER BEGINS

Reluctantly, I returned home and tackled weeks of work that was stacked up. But my return was accompanied by a quiet resolve to take the next step in my inspirational studies by enrolling in Unity's Correspondence Course. Although I had no idea whether I could handle the lessons, I was determined to try. The main problem was time—when would I be able to do the required study?

My hard-working boss thought nothing of our putting in a full day—from 9 A.M. to 5 P.M., five days a week— then asking me to return later, from 7 P.M. until 10 P.M. I also worked half a day on Saturdays, then came back from 7 P.M. until 10 P.M. on Sunday nights. The strength and stamina of youth somehow carried me through. But this schedule meant I had to do correspondence course lessons during the week, in the middle of the night at home, and in the quiet of the public library on Saturday afternoons. But I did them. And though the lessons were slow going, I loved what I was learning.

Furthermore, I discovered that I loved identifying, clarifying, organizing, and setting down my own ideas on paper. Little did I know that my writing career had just begun. To be writing like that was a course of action ultimately destined to become a way of life with me, and it would eventually lead me to have a modest fame-and-fortune image in the eyes of the world, in what was to become a part of my "special and different" way of life.

Later, I also realized that all the hard work and long hours that were expected of me, plus my boss's perfectionism with regard to his paperwork, were but the disciplined steps I needed to take in getting ready for the expanded way of life that lay ahead.

Thus for six summers I went back and forth to Missouri to study. My summers at Unity School consisted not only of intense study but also of personal expansion by way of recreational off-hours and weekend breaks. During those times, I looked forward to visiting Kansas City's various museums, attending its popular Starlight Theater musical productions in Swope Park, where among others, I saw Ethel Merman in *Call Me Madam* and Pearl Bailey in *Porgy & Bess*, and dining on the elite Country Club Plaza.

Then I returned home to continue my studies through the correspondence courses. Although the process seemed just to involve a simple method of inspirational study, it actually was a brilliant way to help students acquire certain on-the-spot training, then use it in their private lives while they continued their studies in whatever fashion their personal and professional lifestyles allowed. It proved to be a far better method for increasing knowledge and promoting inner growth than were the high-pressure, "hot house" methods required of students in some other fields of religion—which often led to a high attrition rate.

UNEXPECTED EVENTS

One spring day, I concluded that I could take no more of the intensity and pressure that were part of my job, especially since the law firm had expanded and several other lawyers and secretaries had been added. When I got up the courage to ask my boss for a raise, he told me in matter-of-fact terms that I was one of the best-paid legal secretaries in town and that I could not do any better elsewhere. In other words, his answer was "no."

Shortly thereafter I got out my Bible, seeking guidance about what to do. It fell open to Acts 26:16: "Behold, I have appeared unto thee for this purpose, to appoint thee a minister and a witness. . . ." (ASV)

Disrespectfully, I slammed my Bible shut and said, "Dear God, if you wanted me to be a minister you should have made me a man. Since you did not, that settles it."

But the restless dissatisfaction continued.

For six years I had returned to Unity School in the summer to study, and I planned to return for a seventh. But after that discouraging conversation with my boss and with summer still two months away, I felt I must immediately take some time off and relax. I could not go on working under that kind of stress without hope of further job expansion or increased financial recognition. And then, amazingly, when I looked at my schedule for the Unity School course of study, I discovered that *spring* classes were being offered—right away.

That gave me the courage to march into my boss's office. I told him I would like to change my usual vacation schedule and take my time off immediately, so I could return to Unity School for more "self-improvement." He knew I was unhappy with our previous conversation, and though he was caught off-guard by my request, he decided to honor it, feeling it would assuage my discontent.

THE PLOT THICKENS

Springtime at Unity School was beautiful. Even more beautiful was the surprising question my Course Advisor asked me: "What are your plans for the future?"

Perplexed, I thought: *"Plans for the future?* How can I answer that? I'm not even sure what my plans for today are."

She continued, "After this term of study, you'll be eligible for consideration to become a licensed Unity teacher/counselor and/or a licensed minister. If you choose the latter and get the required on-the-job training in a church, you could later be recommended for ordination. Regardless of which you might choose, the first requirement would be a year's experience in a Unity church, where you would teach, counsel, and help out as needed."

My mind went blank from shock. I'd been coming here for inspiration and "self-improvement." Then suddenly I wondered: Could this be the beginning of the answer to the question I had been asking myself since childhood about the "special and different" something I was supposed to do in life? Had I been unknowingly preparing for it through my inspirational studies—as well as through the unexpected heartbreaking experiences life had already dealt me?

Suddenly I remembered that Bible verse which I had originally dismissed. "Behold, I have appeared unto thee for this purpose, to appoint thee a minister and a witness. . . ."

As I sat there, silently and swiftly analyzing everything, my Course Advisor continued: "You have all the qualities one needs to become a good minister. But you also have drawbacks. You are a single parent with no independent income. Your youth is also a factor. The Unity founders felt a person should not be considered for the ministry until age forty, or even later. This gave the person time to raise a family and make some money in a business or profession—money he or she would need as a minister, since we have no central funding."

She gave me a searching look, then continued, "Also, few of our churches are in a financial position to provide for a minister-in-training as well as her child. In fact, most of our ministers come out of Unity churches in their own hometown, where they got the required training while working there and living at home. So your situation presents a unique set of problems to be dealt with."

I said nothing. I was still in shock.

Then she went on, "In spite of all the challenges involved, with your permission I'd like to contact the Placement Department and get your name on the list for possible trainee-placement."

Numb from the possibilities she'd raised, I gave her the permission she requested. And she put my name on the list.

Several weeks later, as I was finishing my term of study, I had heard nothing more. When I inquired of my Course Advisor, she contacted the Placement Department again.

The Placement Advisor told her, "After thinking it over and realizing all the obstacles involved, I decided against making any telephone calls." And she added, "There's only one possibility anyway: Unity Church in Birmingham, Alabama. They need a trainee. The present minister is burdened with mail to be answered and classes to be taught, and doesn't have enough help in the counseling ministry. However, it's a small Southern ministry, and I don't see how they could afford Catherine and her son."

My Course Advisor shot back, "Well, at least make a telephone call and give the situation a chance."

Reluctantly the Placement Advisor agreed to do so.

FURTHER DEVELOPMENTS

The next morning the Course Advisor called me into her office for an update. "The minister in

Birmingham remembers you from when she was teaching at Unity School and you were studying there, which is good. But the Placement Department still gave her the names of two other possible trainees. Both of them sound more suitable for that situation. However, the Birmingham minister agreed to go into meditation to get specific guidance, then to call me back."

Considering that only a few weeks before I had no intentions of entering the ministry, this whirlwind situation hardly seemed real to me. Nevertheless, I had actually become excited by the idea of becoming a trainee, but now I was developing some apprehension over the uncertainty that had come up.

Time was running out and I was anxious, as I had only a few days left in my course of study and we were coming down to the wire regarding my official future or non-future with the Unity Movement. So while I waited for the minister in Birmingham to meditate, I began packing to return home, even as I was completing my last days of study.

Then I was summoned to the Course Advisor's office. She said, "The Birmingham minister just called me back. She said it came to her in meditation that you *are* the one to come to Birmingham. She wants you there for an interview as soon as possible."

A chill of exaltation went through me, like nothing I had ever experienced before.

DEFINITE GUIDANCE

In a daze, I started my drive home in the modest little car that had been among my first prosperity demonstrations as a result of my inspirational studies—and also a result of my having begun to tithe ten percent of my gross salary, back when my salary was only $25 a week. Now my father no longer walked the floor and wrung his hands over my taking a bus alone for two days and two nights to Missouri. He had graduated to near hysterics over my driving halfway across the United States alone.

In my desire to get home as quickly as possible before going to Alabama, I drove for twenty-four hours without stopping to eat or sleep—only for gas. Finally, on the second day early in the evening, I was driving through a beautiful mountain area on the home stretch. There I spied a rustic-style restaurant located on the side of the mountain. I decided to give myself a rest break and stopped for an early dinner. This charming restaurant was quiet, with the smell of country ham heavy in the air.

All day I had been praying, "Father, if you really want me to go to Alabama as a start toward a new future, please give me a definite sign. I don't want to go home and upset my boss by asking for more time off—which could mean the loss of my job—in order to check out another job unless I can be sure I'm going to get it. So what is the Truth about this situation? Make it so plain and so clear that I cannot mistake it."

As I relaxed in that mountainside restaurant enjoying a delicious dinner with the feeling of spring in the air, I suddenly realized that music was playing softly in the background. The song? "Stars Fell on Alabama." That was it! Now I knew for sure I was on my way into a new life.

FACING THE MUSIC

With a song in my heart, I returned home to my family and my job. My boss assumed the time away would bring me back happy, renewed, and ready to tackle my job with him again, which is what had always happened in the past. Instead, I said on my first morning back, "Boss, at the end of the day, we need to have a private conference."

I told him what the possibilities were and that I would work overtime to get caught up on the backlog of work in his office before departing for my new job-prospect in Alabama.

He was stunned. "I thought you were doing this special study for 'self-improvement.'"

"And haven't I improved?" I retorted.

In spite of the long hours and the many demands, I had enjoyed working with him. The virtues of his background as a Southern gentleman and his Duke-Harvard education had not been lost on me. I'd appreciated working in an office where profanity, obscenities, and off-color stories or jokes were nonexistent, just as they were at home.

I had always valued pleasantness as the only way to conduct business, and this he had always provided. When he was annoyed with me, he never raised his voice. He only changed his tone, and I knew I had erred. I used the same method on him. No one but the two of us ever knew when dissatisfaction had occurred.

Perhaps what I respected most about him was the way he treated his father. When my boss arrived in the office each morning, he went into his father's office and said, in his usual formal manner, "Good morning, Father." Then they went over the day's agenda. At the end of the day, he always concluded with "Good night, Father."

Toward me, he exhibited that same formal, Southern style, displaying no undue familiarity. As a term of respect, he unfailingly called me "Miss Catherine" in public settings, as did his clients, and he almost always referred to me that way around the office as well.

I knew I had worked for a rare and brilliant man—the likes of which I would probably never see again—who patiently taught me so much. Before his premature death some years later, but after he had observed my progress from afar, he gallantly described me as "the small girl who became a great lady."

LOVE OF THE DEEP SOUTH

When I got to Alabama, I found the Birmingham Church housed in a picturesque old Southern mansion. They called it "Unity in the Deep South."

I visited with the minister—a tall, beautiful, mystical woman—for a day and two nights. She showed me the stack of mail awaiting answers and asked me to sit in on an evening class she was teaching. Afterward, she introduced me to the Board of Trustees. She found a spot upstairs in that delightful old mansion where I could sleep.

Everything felt right. After all the inner turmoil and outer uncertainty of the past several years, I felt at peace—finally.

When she arose with me at 6 A.M. on the last morning of my visit and prayed with me before I departed, her prayers gave me what I needed—for the long day's drive home, for facing the music of leaving a job I had held for almost ten years, and for collecting the few bare essentials I owned and getting back there to Unity in the Deep South by the appointed date, two weeks later—August 1, 1956.

It was a real stretch but I made it. With stars in my eyes and the warmth and beauty of the Deep South in my heart, I was on my way to a brand-new life. I began innocently to declare, "I LOOK WITH WONDER AT THE GOOD THAT LIES BEFORE ME," little suspecting what I was getting myself into!

CHAPTER 5

The Stars Begin To Fall On Alabama

I had naively assumed that folks living in the Deep South all went barefooted, were usually illiterate, and said "git" instead of "get." Was I ever in for a surprise!

In that beautiful old Southern mansion, I met some of the most loving, caring, kind, and considerate people I had ever known. They took me to their hearts immediately.

ACROSS A CROWDED ROOM

In the years after my husband passed on, I had various casual beaus. But once I got interested in my inspirational studies, I took none of them seriously. However, one Sunday morning soon after my August 1956 arrival in Birmingham, I looked across the church's crowded chapel and noticed, sitting there, one of the most attractive men I had ever seen. I was sure I even observed a bright light, a kind of glow, all around him.

As I looked at that man and his movie-star aura, I thought, "That's the first man I've seen in more than fifteen years who is the type that could interest me." But then a quick reality-check produced this additional thought: "I have no time for romance even if he were available, since I'm on my way to becoming a minister. That—along with raising my son—will be a full time job."

After the service, he was introduced to me by a church member as "the favorite son of Unity Church of Birmingham." He had grown up in that church, then served a long stint in the military. Upon his return, he became vice-president of the Board of Trustees. We seldom saw him on Sunday mornings, though, because he was doing graduate work at Birmingham Southern College (now University), and working at night to supplement his income.

He occasionally dropped by the church during the week to pick up literature for his additional inspirational studies, browse in the book room, pay the minister a courtesy call, or leave a tithe offering for the church. I had little personal contact with him during my year-in-training, though toward the end of it he proved influential in helping me professionally.

His name was Kelly Ponder.

UNFORESEEN CHANGES

Unforeseen events lay just ahead. The minister kept me busy helping her answer her backlog of mail as well as doing telephone counseling and monitoring her classes. But she soon informed me that she was scheduled to spend the next month teaching in the Ministerial School at Unity Headquarters and that I would be left to run the day-to-day operations of the church. Thankfully, she had arranged for the few other Unity ministers in the South to come in as Sunday-morning guest speakers. My job was to act as their hostess, arrange for their comfort, and assure that everything ran smoothly during their weekend visits. This meant a seven-day-work-week for me. So what else was new?

Toward the end of the following month, the minister returned from her teaching assignment—only long enough to announce that Unity School had asked her to fill in as Guest Minister for a month at another Unity Church in the South. Conflicts had apparently developed there, and the Placement Department of Unity School felt she had the high-powered prayer and meditation consciousness needed to resolve those problems and get that church ready for its next minister. So off she went again, leaving me to another month of seven-day weeks.

A SPIRITUAL MENTOR

During this time I had the opportunity to get acquainted individually with the members of the Board of Trustees. The one most helpful to me was a man the same age as my father who, over time, became my spiritual mentor—and, in fact, almost was like a father to me. Anytime I had a problem, he would help me pray it into a solution. Since I had never been very close to my own father—which was not unusual in the culture of those times—having understanding and emotional support from both this man and his charming wife was a real bonus.

I particularly admired him because he had gone from rags to riches after the age of fifty. Some years earlier, when he attended his first Unity lecture, the speaker had said, "As you tithe, so you prosper." He recognized the spiritual logic of that, took it to heart, and so became an avid tither. By the time I met him, he had become independently wealthy.

His weekday routine was always the same. He went into downtown Birmingham to check on his investments and other business interests. Then he came by the church to help handle its business and to spend time with me in the Prayer Room. After that he was off to his Country Club for lunch, to play an afternoon of golf with his cronies, and later to arrive home in time for an early dinner with his wife. They both attended bridge tournaments around the country. All of this, plus an occasional vacation trip and regular church attendance, kept them busy.

UNEXPECTED RESULTS

During the month the minister was away helping straighten out that other church, the people there fell in love with her and insisted they wanted her as their minister. When she pointed out that she had to return to her Birmingham church, they paid no attention. Instead they assured her they were going "to pray her back as their minister." They immediately started prayer groups for that purpose.

By the time she returned to Unity of Birmingham, she had been gone two months, and the enthusiasm for her there had waned. She expected to be welcomed back on the job with standing-room-only attendance at her first Sunday service. But it did not happen, nor did it happen with any of her various other activities in the church. Everything was, and remained, very quiet after her return. Meanwhile the prayer groups in that other church continued praying fervently for her to become their minister. The phone calls and letters she got were mostly from her admirers there.

When she told her Birmingham congregation of the strong desires of the *other* congregation to have her as their minister, the Birmingham group seemed neither impressed or concerned.

She began going into meditation more often than usual.

Then one day she received a telephone call from the Placement Department at Unity School. "The people in that church are giving us fits. We have offered them any number of ministers as candidates for their church. They want none of them. They only want you as their minister." The caller continued, "We hope you'll seriously consider this situation. You went in and straightened out a grave problem. They are afraid no other minister can keep things peaceful there, but that you can. Frankly, we feel the same way. We do not know of another minister who has your prayer and meditation consciousness for getting such matters straightened out, then keeping them straight."

Back into meditation she went, sometimes for hours at a time.

Finally she announced to Unity School that she would return to the other church permanently if they would consider sending to Birmingham a certain minister fresh out of Ministerial School whom she felt strongly about, who was then serving a small group in another part of the country. Unity officials objected, feeling he lacked the experience needed. She insisted. When that young minister was contacted by Unity School to determine if he would even consider it, he replied, "Would I? My wife and I have been praying for a larger, more substantial ministry."

The poet Alfred, Lord Tennyson was right. "More things are wrought by prayer than this world dreams of."

The Birmingham minister was gone in a flash. The people in that other church were so delighted to have her back that they rewarded her with a much-needed new car. She filled that little church and had people practically hanging from the rafters for her Sunday and Wednesday services, classes, and counseling appointments. The parking problem created by triumphant attendees became such a nuisance to the neighbors that they complained to the city. That's the kind of problem most ministers pray for!

DEEP SOUTH FEELINGS ASSERTED

Meanwhile, back in Birmingham, our new minister was given a lukewarm welcome. He was considered a "Yankee" in the Deep South of the 1950s, where racial distinctions weren't the only basis for discriminating against people regarded as different. Dislike of the region of the country from which they migrated was also considered a perfectly valid basis for not accepting them. The new minister may not have been born on the wrong side of the tracks, but he certainly had been born on the wrong side of the country—for that group. His ministry was doomed from the start.

When I was approached by his critics, I always said, "He's doing the best he can, so let's pray about it. He's still getting on-the-job training." I did not add, "And so am I."

He lasted until late spring, when the Board of Trustees finally got up the courage to call the Placement Department at Unity School and complain. Their complaints seemed to fall on deaf ears. That is, until Kelly Ponder, Vice-President of the Board of Trustees, got into the act.

First, he made an appointment for an early afternoon visit with the minister—a meeting that went on between the two of them for several hours in the minister's study. After their long visit, they both recognized and acknowledged the man's unsuitability for serving that ministry and agreed he would be happier leaving Birmingham. The minister resigned in that meeting, and then they ended their session in prayer for both his future and that of the church. Within several weeks, he collected his wife and household effects from their rented apartment and left the area. I can only assume that he was as relieved as was everyone else, for he was a young minister who, unfortunately and through no fault of his own, got involved in a situation that was over his head. I felt sad for him and his wife, but I was sure they'd have a better chance in another part of the country.

TO THE RESCUE

The question among the congregation then became "Now what do we do?" Kelly Ponder and my spiritual mentor encouraged the rest of the Board of Trustees to make the decision to ask Unity School to allow me to become their next minister. Usually a trainee was never allowed to continue as minister and was reassigned elsewhere. But this was an unusual situation that called for unusual measures.

Unity School already felt partially responsible for what had developed, since they pulled the original minister out of our church to be a troubleshooter elsewhere at a time when she was doing fine in Birmingham. Also, officials at Unity School tended to listen to Kelly Ponder. He had grown up around Birmingham's Unity Church and knew the types of ministers who had done well there and those who had not. As he pointed out, I was of Southern heritage and had been welcomed into that congregation with much love and appreciation.

The trustees, the congregation, and Unity School all felt I had conducted myself appropriately during that difficult year of training. I personally felt I got more thrown at me than I'd bargained for. However, I was to learn later that the unexpected could be the norm in that type of work. Meanwhile, I kept quiet.

AN ADDITIONAL MANTLE

The final result was that a year after I became a minister-in-training, I returned to Unity School, appeared before their strict Examining Board, and became a Licensed Minister. I was assured that if I did well in my new job, I would be invited to be ordained at their next Ministers' Conference, a year later, in early 1958. And it happened just that way.

Reverend Lowell Fillmore, President of Unity School and son of its founders, did the honors. Since he was the writer in that generation of the Fillmore family, I later felt his ordination of me had carried with it an added blessing—that he had placed the mantle of his writing talent upon me, too.

Only after my ordination did my mother remember a prayer she and my father had prayed before I was born. They had promised God that if He would send them a boy, they would dedicate his life to the ministry. (Many families followed the Southern tradition that a family was expected to produce at least one minister: Baptist and Methodist on my mother's side; Presbyterian and Episcopalian on my father's side.)

Instead, they got me. *They thought their prayers had not been answered.* And when I was ordained, they still thought their prayers had not been answered. My becoming the first lady minister in the family, and of a group with a nondenominational origin, was cause for my mother to object. Citing I Timothy 2:12, she declared, "St. Paul said women were not supposed to speak in the church."

But I was not troubled. In fact, my Bible teacher in ministerial school had once explained that whatever Paul said on that subject was reflecting the culture of his time, when no self-respecting woman would be caught verbally expressing herself in public gatherings. That prohibition was surely never intended to be regarded strictly, as a religious doctrine—though it is regarded that way by some people.

OBJECTIONS OVERRULED

My mother's objection brought back memories of my first visit to that Unity Retreat and our joint reactions thereafter.

Upon my arrival back home, my no-nonsense mother had said, "Daughter, I'm glad you were so impressed with all you found at Unity School. But there must have been something you did *not* like."

Hesitantly, I replied, "Well, Mother, one thing really bothered me about those Unity people. Do you know they have *women ministers?*"

My fiery little mother replied, "That does it. I'll never send Silent Unity another cent."

And she did not.

Until—

Another problem arose in the family. Then she wrote Silent Unity for prayers, as she had so often done in the past.

I suppose the reason my mother and I were so startled to hear of women ministers was that the only women we knew in religious work had always been either Sunday School teachers or missionaries. Women *ministers* seemed a peculiar breed to us, to say the least.

Later, we both had a chance to eat our words. I, of course, did so when I was ordained and became the first lady minister in our family. Then some years later, Mother followed along when she became the first lady elder in her denomination.

By the 1950s, times were changing drastically. One was now hearing the term "Father-Mother God." And women ministers were becoming more accepted by the general public. However, even in those years, my mother and father still continued to have their private doubts.

BOUND FOR THE GREAT SOUTHWEST

When I returned from Unity School as the newly ordained minister, Kelly Ponder informed me that he was leaving for Austin, Texas.

I was surprised. "What's in Austin, Texas?" I asked innocently.

Startled, he replied, "*Only* the University of Texas, Catherine."

I assumed we had just lost a Board member. I further assumed that was the last I would see of or hear from that attractive man.

CHAPTER 6

The Stars That Fell On Alabama Landed

Now that Kelly Ponder had departed, a couple of Board members who had not been among my most enthusiastic supporters decided the time had come to pull rank. It was 1958, and at my first Board meeting in my new job, a man and a woman member objected to my becoming their permanent minister.

"You are too young and inexperienced," he said.

"We want a man as our minister," she complained.

Silently I could not have agreed with them more. But I knew I had to take a stand in my own favor, to establish myself as strong and credible—both as a person and as their minister.

So I replied, "I am not here on a temporary basis. I am here to stay. You may be right about my youth and inexperience. But I was called by the Holy Spirit, trained by Unity School, and invited by you and this congregation to become your minister. I only plan to work with a harmonious Board of Trustees. We've had enough uncertainty and change in this church in recent times. If you wish to help me with this ministry, I invite you to stay. But if you object to me as the minister, I'll be happy to accept *your* resignation, because I'm not going anywhere. Meanwhile, let's pray about it. Furthermore, you are getting a man, because Jesus Christ is the minister of this church, and I am only His representative."

By nightfall on the day of that meeting, the objecting male member had telephoned the chairman of the Board of Trustees and resigned. The contentious woman member resigned by letter several days later.

THE SECRET OF PULLING THINGS TOGETHER

How did I pull that ministry back together? By forming prayer groups that met regularly and quietly to pray for the welfare of that ministry, and by praising and blessing everything that moved. The result was that tithes and offerings started streaming in again.

The bills got paid. Air conditioners and a speaker system were given to us and installed. Our richest member made the church a gift of beautiful ivory-colored chairs for the chapel. Volunteers made gifts of paint for the walls and then became the painters who applied the paint. Troubles of the past were soon drowned out by the progress of the present. What an excited, appreciative, enthusiastic congregation they became!

In that connection, Richard—who was all of nine years old—solved an unexpected problem in his own unique and creative way. Everyone was elated to have an air-conditioned chapel except the lady next door to the church, who had to listen to the hum of the large outdoor compressor. She considered it a nuisance.

Richard soon appointed himself a committee of one to call on her—which he just happened to do near lunchtime. Although surprised by his appearing at her door, she invited him into the kitchen, where she was cooking. He ended up eating lunch with her as well as having his "committee of one" meeting, and they got along famously. Like many diplomats, Richard believed in doing business and eating at the same time whenever possible. They became fast friends, and she no longer complained.

MEETING THE NEXT DEADLINE

My schedule was soon filled with preparation for Sunday morning talks, Monday night and Tuesday morning classes, and midweek Wednesday night services. The phone began to ring off the hook with requests for counseling by telephone and by personal appointment. I set aside one night a week for counseling those who worked during the day.

I employed a part-time secretary to help answer my mail, which came in from all over the South, since I was their nearest Unity minister. At the tender age of thirty, I was ministering to people in at least three Southern states on a regular basis.

I met with all kinds of people. A young Baptist pastor used to sneak in to see me for counseling by appointment after hours, so his own flock would know nothing about it. A college dean of women who'd had an unhappy love affair that ended in a nervous breakdown came from out of state to recover at a relative's home and to receive counseling from me. In a few short weeks, she returned to her job ready to face the world again.

In those still-segregated 1950s, a lady of African-American descent who was highly respected in her community on the other side of town came once a month, after hours, to get two dozen copies of Unity's well-known magazine, *Daily Word.* She rode several buses to get there and always arranged to arrive after the church closed for the day, in order to see me privately. She made that choice to avoid turning occasions of personal counseling into an overt challenge to the community's deeply held attitudes about race. Neither of us was trying to revolutionize the world's racial attitudes. What we *were* trying to do, each of us in our own way, was meet the spiritual and inspirational needs of her followers.

I would like to think our efforts helped improve their situation, both then and later, as we visited, counseled, and prayed together about the fine work she did through her prayer and study group. That quiet, unassuming, but very smart lady experienced miracles among her followers as she led them in the use of life's universal spiritual laws.

For me there were also hospital calls to make, private prayer groups to lead, weddings and christenings to perform, and funeral/memorial services to conduct. My greatest challenge was scheduling—working everything in, doing so in a calm, peaceful way, and non-resistantly meeting the deadlines.

RICHARD'S EARLY DAYS IN BIRMINGHAM

In the midst of all this ongoing activity, my now-ten-year-old son continued—as he always did—to make my life more lively. To begin with, he'd accompanied me to Birmingham kicking and screaming. He hadn't wanted to leave his friends and family back home. Then when he learned we would be living off of "love offerings," he considered it a no-win situation. That we arrived in Birmingham with only $30 in cash had taken nerve. But as Florence Shinn once wrote, "Faith without nerve is dead."[4]

But he understood the circumstances. He knew my income from the business world had just covered our basic necessities and my yearly jaunts halfway across the United States to study at Unity School. And he knew my sudden departure from my hometown job and the

---

4. *The Game of Life and How to Play It*, by Florence Shinn (DeVorss & Co., Marina del Rey, CA 90294).

move to Birmingham had not left me time to recoup financially. He further knew the "call" had been so strong and clear that I felt I had to answer it, money or no money. He may not have agreed with what we were doing, but he did understand.

So we didn't talk to each other a lot about our financial situation, though I suggested we declare prosperity affirmations together daily. Richard agreed to do so, but only for five minutes a day. Very methodically, he timed our affirmation periods. If, at the end of five minutes, we were in the middle of affirming a prosperity statement, it did not matter to him. Off he'd go, feeling he had done his part for the day.

In spite of the brevity of that daily period and his reluctant attitude, we got sufficient financial results to keep the wolf away from the door.

One lady who had a clothing shop often came for counseling about her business. She was not a member of our church, nor did she contribute to it financially. But what she did do was invite Richard and me over occasionally to bless her store after hours. We walked up and down the aisles and, with her, declared prosperity affirmations, after which she helped Richard select the free items of clothing he needed. She always reported increased income after our sessions with her.

Financial needs we didn't anticipate were often met by unexpected love offerings, which usually resulted from my counseling ministry. The uncertainty of this method of developing income could be exasperating to Richard, however.

He once said, "Mother, look at these shoes of mine. The soles are worn out."

I said, "Son, you are right. I am supposed to be in the soul-saving business, but I don't see any salvation for those soles."

The hardest days were those when I had to send him to school without lunch money. But seeing him in later years, one would never know he'd ever missed a meal.

RICHARD'S INVESTIGATIVE ABILITIES

I learned the hard way never to take him with me on an at-home counseling call.

Just as he was returning from school one afternoon, I was on my way out the door to visit a sick church member at her home, and I innocently invited him to join me. We drove to her beautiful residence in an upscale suburb of the city. I left him in the living room while I went into her darkened sickroom to talk and pray with her.

After we finished, as Richard and I were on our way home, he said confidently, "I know the exact cause of her 'sickness.' "

"What do you mean?" I asked in astonishment.

"While you were with her, I checked every trash can in the rest of the house. They were all filled with empty whiskey bottles."

So much for her mysterious illness. And so much for Richard as a companion on counseling calls. I never took him with me on such visits again.

Nevertheless, he made it his job to use his investigative abilities in other ways—again unasked.

On Sunday mornings after the service, Richard made a point of quietly floating around among the members of the congregation as they chatted with one another. The fact that he was doing covert surveillance, listening to the various conversations as he moved about, was never detected. The result? He knew everything that was going on in the church—things people felt I should know about and things people felt I should *not* know about, but which they felt free to discuss among themselves.

Richard then casually offered me the information I was not supposed to know about—for a price. He was what's known as a "paid informer"—long before I'd ever heard of that term. Often I didn't have the money to buy his hot-off-the-press information, so he offered to loan me the money, always at his own interest rates.

Nevertheless, I learned a lot, either about things people were saying behind my back or about situations they wanted me to know nothing about. And they never figured out how I knew. They finally decided I must be "very spiritual," or just plain psychic. In these matters, they came to view me with vast respect, thanks to Richard.

In his defense, I must admit that at times when I was literally down to my last cent, Richard came to my rescue. He always managed to keep a few pennies, nickels, dimes, and sometimes quarters hidden at the church, spread out under one of the thick carpets that people walked on every day. He never hid his valuable backup fund in the same area twice, so not even I could find it. But he always knew exactly where it was in time of need. Could this have been his first step toward later becoming a banker?

HIS FINANCIAL INVESTIGATIVE ABILITIES

Another way he kept tabs on what could have been termed "The Church of What's Happening Now," decades before Flip Wilson publicized it on his hit TV show, was through a tactic that must have frustrated the ushers. He always managed to be with them—uninvited—when they counted the offerings after each class and service.

Furthermore, he kept a running account of what the offering amounts were. Curiosity, of course, had nothing to do with it. He patiently explained to me that he just wanted to be sure the ushers' figures tallied with the financial records they presented. That the ushers didn't appreciate being monitored by a ten-year-old kid who made no secret of the fact that he was checking right behind them—unasked—had to be an understatement.

But they may have changed their minds, if only slightly, when he once came to their rescue. A visiting speaker was in town, and the trustees had agreed to give him a certain fee. After his talk, as they were counting out the offering, they realized they were short of having the needed amount.

So Richard unexpectedly said, "That will never do." He reached into the pockets of his jeans and, from his own funds, took out what was needed, threw it magnanimously on the desk, and said, "Problem solved." He never told me this story, though one of the formerly-irritated-with-Richard ushers proudly related it to me later. The usher admitted that Richard's act of benevolence *did* help lessen the sting of his always being around to check on them.

If storing money under the church carpets didn't plant the seeds of Richard's later career as a banker, then these excursions into the world of tracking income and solving problems with money surely did!

RICHARD'S OTHER FINANCIAL ACTIVITIES

Being a free spirit, Richard got busy making his own circle of friends upon our arrival in town, and he devised his own methods of staying occupied.

Among his friends was a budding artist who lived down the street and helped him to plot and plan things. On one occasion, they took the church's Dial-A-Prayer cards and turned them over, then his friend drew pictures of guns on the back. These drawings were accompanied by the handwritten slogan "Have Gun, Will Travel," taken from the popular television show of that era.

Richard handled the marketing end of their venture. He took the cards and showed them to children at his school, pointing out that each card contained an original drawing, signed by the artist. The cards sold like hotcakes. Richard gave his friend a 10% "artist's fee"—which his friend, who was unsophisticated about the common-sense side of business and finance, was happy to receive. He felt he was well on his way to becoming a successful professional artist.

And that might have happened—except I realized how fast the Dial-A-Prayer cards were disappearing. I couldn't recall that anybody had suddenly shown an inordinate interest in prayer at the church. Then someone found a stray Dial-A-Prayer card on the floor, with that gun drawing and slogan on the back.

When I confronted Richard, he coolly replied, "Mother, you wanted those Dial-A-Prayer cards circulated. I simply figured out how to do it. The drawing was to get their attention. Then, naturally, they turned the card over and got the *real* message."

I appreciated the nobility of his supposed intention but found his methods less than admirable, so that was the end of his experience in the prayer-card business.

He later devised yet another way to make things interesting for me during Sunday services. He always managed to sit in my plain view. When I gave a talk he liked, to show his approval, he smiled and winked at me. When he did not like my talk, he started tapping his watch. If that didn't work, he'd take it off and hold it to his ear. I don't know whether his watch ever actually stopped, but I usually did shortly thereafter—again to keep down the distraction. In that instance, I suspect the congregation appreciated his "help" in getting my Sunday talks concluded.

RICHARD'S SPORTS ACTIVITIES

During his Birmingham days, Richard enjoyed participating in many types of sports activities—among them football, basketball, Little League baseball, golf, tennis, and even Ping-Pong.

He learned to play golf with one club and one ball, which he practiced using in the park below where we lived. On rainy days, when he couldn't get outside, he often amused himself by using the wide hallway upstairs in that Southern mansion to play a somewhat restricted version of the game.

As for baseball, he frequently gathered the neighborhood kids together and had a game in the front yard, outside the church, while I worked on a talk in the church study or did research. A consequence of this was that I gave one usher the job of arriving early on Sunday mornings just to be sure no leftover equipment from Richard's ball games was in the front yard for anyone to see—or *not* see, and then trip over. I'm glad I couldn't hear what the ushers must have said among themselves about Richard's freewheeling method of organizing sports events.

(However, his various ways of making the ushers feel needed scarcely compared to the activities of one young member of our Sunday School. This fellow always came to church accompanied by a screwdriver. He fancied himself a mechanic, and busily tried to prove it by removing doorknobs when nobody was looking. *Two* ushers had to be assigned to him, so the rest of us could stay a step ahead of his engineering antics. Who says being involved in churchwork is dull?)

A SPECIAL VISIT

Among Richard's most memorable experiences in sports was the time his Birmingham basketball team earned a place in the championship playoffs in Montgomery, the state capital. While he was there, Richard and another basketball player decided to pay an unannounced visit to the state's chief executive, Governor John M. Patterson (who held that post just prior to the outspoken, frequently controversial George Wallace).

When Richard and his friend went to the governor's office, the governor's secretary asked the nature of their business. Richard announced proudly, "We are among the championship basketball players, here for the playoffs. I'm sure the governor will want to see us."

The secretary was so impressed with these two nervy kids in their jeans who just showed up in the chief executive's office that she ushered them in to see the governor. Using his instincts as a successful politician, he treated them like the visiting dignitaries they considered themselves to be.

Richard continued playing tennis and golf into his adulthood. He developed a three handicap in golf and probably could have played professionally. In fact, several pro golfers became his good friends.

AN ANALYSIS OF THIS ERA

Among the most notable features of Richard's years in Birmingham was probably not so much that he survived his childhood there, but that those around him—whose lives he made so "interesting"—did!

Nor were his gifts for stirring up the lives of the people around him limited to Birmingham. When he spent his summers back home with my family and his friends—a time his Granny always looked forward to eagerly—he had ample opportunity to share with an entirely different group of people his talent for livening things up.

On occasion, even if they didn't say the words out loud, I recognized that some of my congregants, colleagues, and even a few friends wondered why I didn't do more to try to control Richard. My unspoken answer was always that he was a unique individual on his own path—which was often more boisterous than some people appreciated. But I felt he should, within the general guidelines I taught him, have the opportunity to be fully and freely himself, to express his spirited way of being. In fact, his lively way of embracing life frequently inspired others nearby to enjoy their own lives a little more.

Furthermore, having an independent-minded, self-sufficient son was a wonderful blessing for me, since it precisely fit my own needs as a minister who had many time-consuming responsibilities. At times, I recalled the statement attributed to President Theodore Roosevelt, whose daughter was likewise a free spirit who was reported to have kept everyone around her jumping. "I have discovered," he said, "that I have one of two choices. I can either concentrate on doing my job or try to deal with my daughter, but I can't do both."

My sentiments, exactly.

CHAPTER 7

A Launching Pad Into The Future

When the stars fell on Alabama, they did not fall gently or land softly. Yet the events that were launched there resulted in blessings I was to enjoy for the rest of my life.

In the days before Alabama's image was associated with segregation conflicts, Birmingham was known as "the magic city." It certainly proved to be so for me then—as it has for many other people since that era.

MY FINANCIAL REQUEST

After many years back home of handling my boss's corporate trust fund checkbook (which never contained less than $100,000) and keeping it straight, I was startled by the fuss the Board members in Birmingham made over management of the church's monthly income. It was a mere pittance compared to what I'd handled while I was in the business world. Still, I was grateful that I was no longer required to be involved in corporate financial mechanics and that I was free to act exclusively in the capacity of a spiritual leader. I was, however, concerned that my personal church income—though insignificant in amount—was a matter of public record in their monthly reports, thus constituting what I regarded as an invasion of my personal privacy.

So in one of my prayerful conversations, I said, "Look here, God. You got me into this. This was Your idea, and we have both moved heaven and earth to get me to this point. Surely you don't want me to starve. And neither do I care for my personal financial status to be a matter of public record, discussion, or debate. It should be a private matter between You and me. If you want me to do Your work, then I suggest You devise a method to provide for me financially in such a way that neither a Board of Trustees nor a congregation is involved. How you manage that is Your concern." Then I released the matter, pending further developments.

They came in a most unexpected way.

A PREMONITION?

Someone has said that ministers try to resign every Saturday night while they are slaving away over their Sunday talks. One such Saturday night, after an exhausting week, I was in full sympathy with that statement as I worked in my study. I put my head on my desk and said, "Dear God, is this all there is? Constant deadlines, constant work, constant fatigue, no time or money for anything?" Suddenly I got an inner flash in which I saw a stack of books thrown together, one on top of the other, in a casual way. They were placed on a no-nonsense straight-backed chair. That was all. No explanation.

Somehow I felt it didn't refer to reading books. It referred to *writing* books.

I thought, "What kind of answer is that? I don't know how to write books, and where would I ever get the time if I did know how? I've written articles for various publications, but even that has been extremely time-consuming. I have no inherited writing talent and no ghostwriter except the Holy Ghost. So this doesn't make any sense." I dismissed that flash as a Saturday-night panic attack.

Then a strange thing happened on my way to not writing books.

FROM RECESSION TO ABUNDANCE

The Recession of 1958 hit Birmingham hard. That city of steel mills had been called "the Pittsburgh of the South," and it was, in fact, named for another steel producing city—Birmingham, England.

A feeling of gloom hung in the air, and the city was finally declared a disaster area, making it eligible for Federal aid. The effect of the recession on our church was significant, as contributions from congregants dropped, and I began to wonder how the church would survive.

Then two ladies asked me innocently, "Doesn't this teaching say that all people can be prosperous . . . as part of our spiritual heritage?"

"Yes, of course," I replied.

"Then why don't you conduct a prosperity class?"

I hesitated, feeling I didn't know enough about the subject. But I was also aware of the long-recognized truth that "we teach what we want to learn," so I ordered all the books I could find on the subject and made Charles Fillmore's book *Prosperity*[5] our basic text.

When the first class of fifty people gathered, they seemed somehow to feel *guilty* about attending a prosperity class. Most came from religious or family backgrounds which taught that being poor was pious and being prosperous could be sinful.[6] But they were depressed, even desperate, and so was I.

---

5. *Prosperity*, by Charles Fillmore (Unity School of Christianity, Unity Village, MO 64065).

6. For a detailed explanation, see *The Dynamic Laws of Prosperity*, by Catherine Ponder (1962; revised edition, 1985, DeVorss & Co., Marina del Rey, CA 90294), chapter 1, "The Shocking Truth about Prosperity."

Yet from the moment we started opening each class with spoken prosperity statements, I recognized that an uplifted feeling began to rise among the class members. Our basic affirmation, which I have used daily ever since, was: "I DO NOT DEPEND UPON PERSONS OR CONDITIONS FOR MY PROSPERITY. GOD IS THE SOURCE OF MY SUPPLY, AND GOD PROVIDES HIS OWN AMAZING CHANNELS OF SUPPLY TO ME NOW." When the class members spoke those words in unison, they lightened and brightened.

As our weekly prosperity classes continued, the attendees began not only to look better and feel better, but they also began to get results.[7]

Two secretaries received raises in pay, one with a promotion and new title. A stockbroker reported that he had more business than he had dared hope for, though most of his fellow brokers were comparatively idle. One client whom he had not seen for several years appeared and handed him a check for $200,000 to invest! A month later, the broker's income was four times its usual amount.

A lawyer in the class who had several industrial clients on strike or out of work reported that the recession was suddenly over for him. His income zoomed upward, growing by $2000 per month, which at that time was a great increase. A steel manufacturer's agent, whose business was strongly affected by recession, reported that he unexpectedly received an order amounting to $4500—a tremendous sum in 1958 dollars—which he had not even solicited.

One woman was a saleslady in a department store that employed over 100 people. At the end of her first

---

7. For details of the teachings and methods offered in those classes, see *The Dynamic Laws of Prosperity*, by Catherine Ponder.

month in our prosperity class, this woman, out of those 100-plus employees, was the only one who received a commission check for having exceeded her monthly quota.

The owner of an electrical business had a large account owing his company that was long overdue. The account was abruptly paid.

A family, burdened with indebtedness, suddenly inherited a considerable sum of money. A telephone company employee got a raise that had been promised months earlier. A construction engineer was given a new assignment, involving a multimillion dollar job out of state (it came so suddenly that he had to leave before the class was completed). One couple even received an all-expense-paid trip abroad!

My son and I, who had been living in a single room in that Southern mansion, were soon provided with a brand-new church manse in one of the city's most prestigious neighborhoods.

And these are but a few examples of the prosperity that came to class members (and their teacher).

FROM RECESSION TO WHOLENESS

The word "prosper" at its root means "wholeness," and various members of the class received their prosperity in the form of something other than monetary wholeness. In particular, they found wholeness that was emotional and physical. One businessman had been told he had a serious heart condition, which required that he be treated constantly. As he relaxed during that prosperity class, his doctor stated that his earlier trouble had vanished. Several people with nervous conditions found new serenity and peace of mind—and therefore better health overall.

One lonely businesswoman who had often threatened suicide became so intensely involved in the teachings of this prosperity class that she reversed her tendency to be self-involved, found interests outside herself, and started leading a happier, more balanced life. Two secret drinkers, a man and a woman, began resolving and dissolving inner hostilities and conflicts. Their drinking gradually diminished and finally stopped.

Marriages were saved after one or both marriage partners attended our class. One person's divorced partner even returned, and they were remarried. Several lonely, unmarried people happily married. One lady who had been widowed for twenty years got married. The word "wealth" in its root means "well-being"—and these people proved it.

THE BUSINESSMEN WHO HELPED ME

As the class members began to share, both publicly and privately, what happened with them, they requested that I write a book about the results they got and the prosperity teachings that had led to those results. My mentor agreed to meet me daily in the church Prayer Room to pray about this possibility. As we did, the chapters for the book began to unfold to me mentally, in an orderly sequence. The stockbroker in the class gave the book its name. I wanted to call it *The Laws of Prosperity*. He said, "No, it is *The Dynamic Laws of Prosperity*, because we have gotten dynamic results." A member of the class who was in the public relations business got busy locating a New York literary agent for me. The agent, in turn, found a publisher—the same publisher who had also made Dr. Norman Vincent Peale's books bestsellers.

STAFF RESULTS

A personal secretary I hired to type the manuscript used the ideas in it—and her husband prospered so much in his sales work that she no longer needed the job! A second secretary typed the rest of the book, but she too resigned, because her husband, who had been out of work when she started typing the book, had gotten the finest engineering job of his life—which took them both out of state.

My housekeeper, who had not attended the class or seen the manuscript, asked me to explain it to her. As I innocently did so, she began using the ideas. She finally said, "I've decided to do something I've always wanted to do and become a dressmaker. So I am resigning as your housekeeper. Do you want me to become your dressmaker?"

I finally learned that if I wanted to keep a staff, I had better keep quiet about that prosperity class and its teachings.

OUR GO-CART CHRISTMAS

What I did not count on in the midst of all these prosperity results was that my own son, now approaching his teenage years, would get into the act—though I should have known by then to expect it! But he wasn't even attending our prosperity class, so he really caught me by surprise.

Christmas was fast approaching and I was apprehensive because I didn't have any money for his Christmas gifts—and he knew it. (When we moved into the church manse, the maintenance and upkeep expenses substantially increased our living expenses, and my income hadn't yet caught up.) Undaunted by this fact, Richard had developed great expectations, as do most children at that time of the year. For months he had been viewing a little gasoline-powered go-cart on display at a nearby hardware store. He had been telling his friends that this machine would be his for Christmas. He even invited all the neighborhood children to come by on Christmas morning for a ride in the go-cart.

Since I did not regard this luxury toy as a reason to start purchasing things on long-term credit, we had two options—pay cash now or no go-cart. Though I had affirmed that divine abundance would manifest in the matter, no extra cash had appeared by the beginning of Christmas week.

My son was unimpressed by this, however. He was busy clearing an area in the garage where he could keep the little machine.

Rather weakly, I inquired how he could be so sure he would get the go-cart as a Christmas gift. He replied, "Mother, I am practicing what *you* teach. I have affirmed that the cart is coming to me in God's own wonderful way. Months ago, I placed a go-cart on my Wheel of Fortune, and I've been picturing it parked in the garage.[8] I've even pictured myself riding it all over the neighborhood." He then gave me a dose of my own medicine. "Don't worry, Mother. Everything will work out! The picturing power of the mind is taking care of this."

After that conversation early in Christmas week, I finally released the matter into Higher Hands. Then, several days later, I unexpectedly received a Christmas gift—of some cash. At first I thought our prayers had

8. The author's prosperity books present detailed information about the picturing power of the mind, including how making a Wheel of Fortune, a Treasure Map, or a Prayer Map can lead to results.

been answered, but when I counted the money, my heart sank. It was $80 less than I needed for Richard's much-desired toy vehicle.

But still, I was grateful for the money, thinking it would cover various other needs nicely. My son, however, seemed to think we had enough money for *his* particular need, even after I explained that we still were short by $80.

He merely replied, "Our prayers have been answered. Let's go down and see about the go-cart."

Late that afternoon, when I could stall no longer, we drove to the store through heavy holiday traffic. As we joined the crowd inside, I allowed myself to be led over to the much-discussed go-cart, which was on display.

As I stood there trying to fully appreciate this little machine, I suddenly became aware that a man was talking quietly to me. At first I assumed that he was a sales clerk. But as he continued speaking, I realized that was hardly possible. He was saying, "Lady, that's a fine little go-cart. If you are interested in getting one for your son, I know where you can get one wholesale. It is available for $80 less than this one, but it is basically the same cart."

In stunned silence, I listened as he explained that one had been ordered for his son by a business friend, but his son had changed his mind. This man, who introduced himself as a local insurance executive, said he had just returned to this store to purchase the bicycle his son actually wanted. However, he felt he was still financially responsible for the go-cart that his friend had ordered at a discount price as a special favor to him.

On the reverse side of one of his business cards, he wrote the name and address of the store where we could find the go-cart. Richard and I quickly made our way there, where we found the little cart, still in its original factory packaging. The owner seemed quite happy to sell it to us at the wholesale price.

No toy was more thoroughly enjoyed by Richard— or by the other kids in the neighborhood—that Christmas morning. We have often referred to that memorable experience as our "go-cart Christmas."

A COSMIC CORRESPONDENCE

All the while Kelly Ponder was at the University of Texas, he continued a practice he developed years before—corresponding with the minister of his home church in Birmingham. His letters always included tithe offerings as well as interesting updates on his life.

His great concern, he told me, was that there was no Unity church in Austin, the state capital. In one of his notes, he asked, "What can I do to get a minister here to start a Unity group?"

"Write Unity School," I advised.

He took my advice, and the School replied that they would be glad to send a minister when Kelly could guarantee a minister an income.

He wrote me, "I can't do that. Now what do I do?"

I suggested, "Start a prayer and study group in order to build a foundation for a ministry. Then use a specific prayer: *Jesus Christ in the midst of this study group now draws to Himself His own divinely appointed minister to develop Unity in Austin.*"

He took that suggestion too, and from the time he did, I began to get restless and did not know why. His study group met off and on for several years. Then he got so busy at the University that he disbanded the group. Besides, nothing seemed to have happened with regard to the founding of a ministry, so he assumed that the group's prayers had not been answered.

But the timeless axiom was no less true: "There must be an *in*working before there can be an *out*working." He simply did not yet realize what his study group had been accomplishing on an inner level.

A COSMIC CONSCIOUSNESS EXPERIENCE

For five busy years, I worked nonstop, around the clock, doing my best to serve, help, and please many people. It was a ministry of constant demands and activities, most of which I fully enjoyed. It was labor, but a labor of love. I had no time or money for vacations, or days off to rest. Even though I might have appreciated those luxuries, I loved the work I was doing—whether or not I had any of the "benefits" that are more common these days.

At that time, I was also writing, chapter by chapter, *The Dynamic Laws of Prosperity* and trying to meet a publisher's deadline. But as time progressed, I began to feel very tired, even burned-out. Yet I *had* to keep going, because I had to make a living for my son and me. Further, there was no one to relieve me in the work of that ministry.

So I asked my prayer mentor to begin declaring with me daily in the Prayer Room: "I AM NOW SHOWN NEW WAYS OF LIVING AND NEW METHODS OF WORK. I AM NOT CONFINED TO THE WAYS AND METHODS OF THE PAST." We continued to declare: "JESUS CHRIST IS IN CHARGE OF THIS MINISTRY."

As we prayed daily for guidance, I began to feel my energy becoming even more depleted. That seemed strange, since prayer usually energized me.

I also began to see a bright inner light that gradually increased in intensity over a period of weeks, until I felt as though I was almost blinded. I had difficulty getting notes together for my talks, or delivering them. At the same time, my throat,[9] an area that wisdom teachers have long considered to be a seat of creative power in the body, became more and more congested until finally, talking became quite difficult for me.

Since it was the spring of the year, I began taking time to sit outside in the sunshine, to soak up its energy and to enjoy the beautiful flowers, shrubs, and sounds of birds singing around me. I said nothing to anyone about my unusual inner experiences, but tried to act as though everything was fine. I continued with my work, bright light and all, though when it was at its fullest, I was inwardly almost blinded by its brightness. Then gradually it began to subside, and over a number of weeks I slowly returned to normal. Who realized I was having that strange experience and who didn't? I'll never know, but anyone who did notice never mentioned it in my presence.

I had felt like St. Paul being struck down on the road to Damascus, when he too saw a bright light, and he too was temporarily blinded. Dr. Richard M. Bucke, in his book *Cosmic Consciousness*[10] a hundred years ago, described this as an experience that is not unusual for spiritually minded people. Maybe not. But for me, it was quite frightening. If I had tried to explain it, who would have believed me?[11]

---

9.   *The Healing Secrets of the Ages*, by Catherine Ponder (1967, DeVorss & Co., Marina del Rey, CA 90294), chapter 6, "Your Healing Faculty of Power."

10.   *Cosmic Consciousness*, by Richard Maurice Bucke, M.D. (1901; 1991, E. P. Dutton & Co., Inc., New York).

11.   *The Dynamic Laws of Prayer*, by Catherine Ponder (1987, DeVorss & Co., Marina del Rey, CA 90294), the chapter titled "The Prayer for Miracles."

But the experience itself was just a beginning. When it was finally over and I was back to normal, amazing things started to happen.

A COSMIC INVITATION

In a matter of weeks, the day came when, out of the blue, I received an invitation to spend a week at Unity of Houston, Texas, dedicating their new building by presenting my prosperity teachings. That invitation came as a result of my having begun to write prosperity articles for several publications. Those articles brought many invitations from my peers to speak on the subject of prosperity. Since the dedication was a summer event, at a time when my son would be back home visiting my parents, I was free to accept.

When next I wrote to Kelly Ponder, I suggested that he bring members of his study group to my Houston lectures, since the distance from Austin to Houston was less than 200 miles.

He wrote back, "I have a better idea." Explaining that many of his study group members worked and couldn't get away for a trip to Houston, he offered an alternative suggestion. "Why don't you first come to Austin, to vacation for a few days? That will give me a chance to show you around the capital city of Texas. You can see for yourself why Unity should have a church here."

I enthusiastically agreed, and we developed a plan for me to drive to Austin for a few days of rest before beginning my strenuous week of work at Unity of Houston.

I had never visited the great state of Texas. When I told my Birmingham congregation I was going there to lecture on prosperity, they were amused. "With all their oil wells and a wealth of cattle, how can those Texans possibly need to hear someone from Alabama talk about prosperity? Aren't you 'carrying coal to Newcastle'?"

We all laughed, since my congregants knew by then that I was going to follow my inner guidance, whatever it was—which, from my viewpoint, meant I would be headed in the right direction.

When I began driving out of Alabama toward Texas, a car flew by me, honked its horn, and the driver waved. That car, ironically, bore a Texas license plate. It portended future events that would have long-lasting effects on my life and on the lives of many others.

CHAPTER 8

The Heart-Of-Texas Saga Begins

On my way to Texas, I stayed overnight with a friend I'd met several years earlier. Her husband had recently passed on, and she was glad to have someone to talk shop with. She also invited the guest minister of her church, another friend of mine, to drop by. He told me he was between churches and waiting for the right place to open up. I declared for him, THE TRUE PLACE, TRUE PEOPLE, AND TRUE PROSPERITY COME QUICKLY, EASILY, AND IN PEACE. I released it and thought no more about it.

After I left, and as I drove into Texas for the first time, I noticed that the shrubs and greenery were of a different variety from what I had always seen in the South. I also realized they were not new to me. I had been seeing them in dreams.

"Strange," I thought, but dismissed the apparent coincidence.

THE MAJESTIC SETTING

The skyline of Austin was beautiful, with the University of Texas tower and its many red-tile-roofed buildings also rising high over the area. The magnificent, pink-granite State Capitol loomed large in the background. "What a majestic setting," I mused.

Later, after I arrived at my motel near the University, Kelly Ponder picked me up for dinner, as he was to do each night I was there. During the days, while he worked, I relaxed by the pool and began to feel the fatigue of many years slowly fading away. It was a quiet, relaxing, satisfying time for me.

Over the weekend, he showed me around town and drove me out into the famed Texas hill country, with its many lakes. It was all very scenic and impressive. He eventually took me by his small bachelor's apartment near the State Capitol and introduced me—not to his friends at first, but to the many books on his shelves there. Most had titles I did not recognize, but all were, according to Kelly, inspirational classics. He was right, and I would hear about many of them for years to come. A number of those books were written by authors he had sought out while he was a military officer, traveling the world. He thus opened my mind to new dimensions of teachings and literature that went far beyond the inspirational materials with which I was already familiar. It was a mind-stretching experience.

And he made his other point completely. By showing me beautiful Austin, Texas, he awakened me to the possibilities there for a Unity Church. Furthermore, my strong attraction for this incredible man was hard to ignore. However, I knew he had never married and that his family felt he was too much of a perfectionist for anyone to interest him seriously. On the other hand, I myself had been unmarried and extremely busy for—how long was it now?—about fifteen years. After that long, romance seemed out of the question for me. So I dismissed my time with Kelly Ponder as a nice experience that would go nowhere.

By that time I was fully relaxed and getting my second wind, which had been my main purpose for this easygoing visit.

WONDERS NEVER CEASE

One evening toward the end of my visit, Kelly said, "Tomorrow night I must talk to you seriously about some things."

I thought, "Here we go again on the Austin pitch for a minister."

However, the next night when he picked me up for dinner, he immediately said, "I have an important question I must ask you. It's one I've never asked anyone before."

"Hmmm. . . ," I thought.

"Will you marry me?"

Stunned and shocked, I nevertheless found myself replying directly, as though it had been scripted, "Yes, I'll marry you. But on one condition."

"What's that?"

"That we get married in two weeks, as soon as I finish my work for Unity in Houston."

Now it was his turn to be stunned and shocked. "*Two weeks?* How can we get married in just two weeks?"

"I don't know. But unless we get married then, too many things could happen that might keep us apart later. So it has to be in two weeks or not at all."

I was remembering my marriage experience of so many years earlier, when I hadn't known how to seize the moment, when I let too many people get into the act and almost ruin my life. They certainly helped ruin that marriage. I didn't dare take such a chance again.

Kelly Ponder, who no doubt had an impressive track record for dodging eligible ladies, finally caught his breath and said, "*Two weeks?* I'll have to *pray* about that."

I left his reaction alone, though I privately thought, "Some proposal. That man takes his religion too seriously."

On the last night of my visit, before I departed for my heavy schedule at Unity of Houston, he picked me up for dinner. When he saw me, the first words out of his mouth were, "Catherine, you are right. I prayed about it, and either we get married in two weeks or we don't get married at all."

I breathed easier. What a relief!

And so we started planning how we could work it out. I immediately remembered the between-churches minister I'd seen on my way to Texas. I telephoned him, asking him to get to Birmingham as soon as possible as a Guest Minister, so he could determine whether he would want to work there permanently—given, of course, the approval of the authorities at Unity School and the members of our Board of Trustees.

Kelly telephoned his sister, who was to become my lifelong friend. She was so relieved that she cried on the phone, since she had given up hope of ever seeing her brother happily settled down. She helped him plan his visit to see the Ponder family that weekend, who now lived on the Texas coast, having migrated there from Birmingham. His delighted family made arrangements for our quiet wedding in their local Protestant church.

Though the marriage may have seemed sudden, it had been coming on for some time. His sister later told me she had known for several years that Kelly wanted to marry me, but couldn't quite figure out the logistics of it all.

HOUSTON

The arrangement was that while in Houston, I would be the house guest of a longtime friend from Birmingham who had married a Houston business-man. I moved into their lovely home for my busy time there. Along with conducting Sunday and Wednesday services, I had classes to teach, a funeral to conduct, counseling to do, and even a Chamber of Commerce breakfast to attend. Since my Houston hostess had grown up with Kelly at Unity of Birmingham, she happily shopped with me and helped me prepare to get married. It all went like clockwork.

My family back home was as shocked as was the Ponder family. They felt, after my heartbreaking early marriage and my entry into the ministerial/writing field, that I would almost certainly not marry again. Until this point, I had assumed they were right.

Nevertheless, on a beautiful summer day, Kelly Ponder and I were married in a charming little Texas church. We later learned that the minister who married us was the cousin of another minister with the same last name who, against all odds, lived in my hometown more than a thousand miles away and was someone my mother knew. Small world. Good world.

Kelly and I didn't walk down the aisle in the customary fashion. He unexpectedly grabbed my hand and practically dragged me down the aisle in his rush to the altar.

I mumbled, "Why the hurry?"

His reply: "Because I've waited all my life for this moment."

AUSTIN

Back in Austin, Kelly and I realized we'd need to get a larger apartment, but not before I fulfilled lecture commitments at three Unity Churches on the famous Gold Coast of Florida—commitments I'd made months before.

In the meantime, while Kelly completed some work assignments during the following few weeks, I slept around the clock for the first time in years. Rest, at last. My prior feelings of burn-out were replaced with a renewed sense of well-being, an indescribable happiness for the present, and great hope for the future. My personal life was finally beginning to make sense.

And Kelly! What an incredible husband he turned out to be! He'd been well worth waiting for—even though I didn't know I'd been waiting. He was among the few people ever to validate my maverick ways. He was the first to say, "Catherine, you are such a pretty little thing." And, "I am so proud of what you've accomplished." And, "I am in awe of your bright mind." My astonished reaction to his many kind words and thoughtful acts was, "So this is what marriage is supposed to be like."

FLORIDA

We spent six weeks in the Palm Beach area while I fulfilled my commitment to act as Guest Minister at three churches so their ministers could vacation. Kelly helped me by acting as Platform Chairman and in various other ways. I conducted Sunday services at one church, Wednesday and Thursday night services at the two other churches, and arranged my days so I could do counseling at all of the churches.

We didn't care for the crowded living arrangement that had been provided for us, so I said to Kelly, "Let's drive up and down County Road on Palm Beach and see what might be available there." I felt that area was where we'd be happiest during the forthcoming six weeks. I added, "It's the Law of Saturation at work."[12]

---

12. For further insight into the Law of Saturation, see *The Prosperity Secret of the Ages*, by Catherine Ponder (1964, DeVorss & Co., Marina del Rey, CA 90294), chapter 11, "The Success Law of Joy and Beauty."

In spite of all his studies over the years, the Law of Saturation was new to him. Thus he considered the action I was requesting to be a waste of time, but he humored me.

That night, after a midweek service, a businessman approached us and said, "I've been reading your prosperity articles in the Unity publications. I don't attend this church, since I'm an official at the Episcopal Church on Palm Beach, but I wanted to hear you speak.

"Also, I'm in the real estate business and this is our slow season, and I have an empty duplex apartment on Palm Beach that is available. Would you like to use it as my guest while you are here? The owners won't return until the winter season."

Kelly was astonished to hear this offer. So, even, was I—though I wasn't really surprised. I had come to expect such miracles.

The realtor didn't have to ask twice and we didn't delay very long before conditionally saying yes. He immediately took us over and through the apartment, where our "conditional" turned into "definitely." We moved in the next day and lived there happily for the following six weeks, between Lake Worth and the Atlantic Ocean. Another majestic setting. The Law of Saturation had done its perfect work quickly.

That realtor and his wife insisted upon acting as our hosts during our stay. For fun, they drove us around Palm Beach in an antique Rolls Royce convertible, and we dined with them in our spare time at the one private club that remained open during the summer. It was a busy, happy time for us.

One of the ministers I was replacing, upon returning from vacation, insisted that I spend one night a week acting as her prayer partner. Toward the end of our first meeting, she said, "We've prayed about what's on my mind. Now what's on *your* mind? What do we need to pray about for *you?*"

I responded immediately, "Only that I need to return to Austin and found a new ministry, and I haven't a clue where to start. Also, I have no money with which to begin it." As we prayed, the name of one lady I'd heard of before—a lady who had once attended Kelly Ponder's study group—kept coming to me. That was the only answer I got.

LAUNCHING A NEW LIFE

After completing our busy but delightful six-week working honeymoon in the Palm Beach area, our first job back in Austin was to find the larger place to live we needed, so Richard could join us. Through newspaper ads, we were guided to a very large apartment, one that was almost as big as some houses. It was located atop a hill overlooking the University of Texas. This proximity to the University meant Kelly could walk back and forth to teach and to do research at the library, without the hassle of traffic. The apartment was large enough for me to reserve room for my work and for counseling appointments.

After getting settled, I contacted the lady whose name had come to me in those Florida prayer sessions. She informed me that she had been keeping some money in a savings account to help start a Unity church in Austin, and that she would send me a check. Her generous gift, plus the offerings I had received in Houston and Florida, helped us launch Unity of Austin.

Our first meetings were held at the historic Driskill Hotel. Its stately columns and wide, gold, Maximilian-styled mirrors from Mexico instantly conveyed a sense of being caught up in the mystique of the Old West, with accompanying flavors of Mexico. At our initial gathering in those elegant chandeliered surroundings, the 150 people crowded into that small ballroom gave Kelly and me a standing ovation when we walked in. To us, it felt like 1500. The welcoming atmosphere of that balmy autumn night only added to the joy everyone was feeling.

Kelly, in his opening remarks, said, "I couldn't get Unity School to send us a minister for Unity here in the capital city of Texas. So I solved the problem on my own. I just went out and married one!" Those Texans laughed and applauded appreciatively. What a send-off, Texas style.

Since Austin was described as "the education center of the Southwest," with about thirty colleges in nearby surroundings, we had many attendees from the field of education in our Unity group. They told me they loved my bookish research, and they frequently took notes on my lectures. Generally conservative and well-to-do, they tended to be reserved and have little to say—though they just kept coming and taking notes.

A private prayer group was formed that quietly met at our apartment once a week to help us pray Unity of Austin into growth and expansion. Our prayer efforts there produced very gratifying results.

And what was Richard doing all this time? He was attending Austin Junior High School, which was near-by. He got a paper route and, in addition, worked at a local gas station to make his own spending money. Still later, he kept busy at Austin High School as the school photographer. In his new life, Richard was a very busy young man.

TESTINGS AND REWARDS

It was a time of testing for my prosperity consciousness, since attendees were inclined to feel that just their presence at those lectures was a satisfactory substitute for actual presents to the ministry. So I made a treasure map, picturing the sums of money we needed for operational expenses.

Within a month after I began teaching the spiritual laws of prosperity, the first $50 bill showed up in the offering, and the ushers were shocked. Within two months, the first $100 bill appeared there, and the ushers were even more shocked. As I persisted in teaching those laws, people gradually began to tithe—and the financial strain we were experiencing lessened significantly.

Meanwhile, my New York publisher was pushing me hard to complete *The Dynamic Laws of Prosperity,* a process that involved—as I was to learn—their asking me to edit it down by half. I howled. The very *idea*!

Kelly said diplomatically, "Let me take a look at it." Without a word, he and his Phi Beta Kappa mind got busy cutting it down to a more practical and usable size. The success of that book became his legacy to me, which has continued ever since.

His further gifts to me were many, and of many kinds. In a personal sense, he delighted in shopping with me and for me. He bought me my first mink jacket and gave me my first Chanel #5 perfume. He took me from homemade dresses to designer clothes—only a few, though always just the right ones. But the way I became really convinced that he loved me was that he ate my cooking—since I can't cook!

Even though I reminded him of what my sister always said—"Catherine's idea of a kitchen is that it's the room you go through on your way to the back door"—it mattered not to him. He often proudly said to whoever would listen, "Catherine's been in the kitchen rattling the pots and pans."

Usually, however, his references to me were more sedate, less dramatic. Frequently, for instance, he referred to me proudly as his "quiet girl."

A BRAZEN REQUEST

Soon after *The Dynamic Laws of Prosperity* was published, I received a request that astonished me. A businessman boldly wrote, "Now that you have written that best-selling prosperity book, that means you are rich, though I am poor. So please send me $50,000, because I need it and you'll never miss it."

I was so astounded that I totally disregarded his request at first. Later I thought, "Wait a minute. If that man wants $50,000, of course I'll send him $50,000."

And I did.

In play money.

Can you blame me for being indignant when that man never even had the courtesy to write me a thank-you note?

I doubt seriously that he got the underlying prosperity message, either—about the power of picturing.

OUR LOCAL SETTING

When the ballrooms of the popular Driskill Hotel became routinely booked by convention groups, we needed to move our Unity of Austin lectures to a more permanent location—the Commodore Perry Hotel. They had just redecorated and were glad to have us. We gradually moved from their smallest, to their midsize, and finally to their largest ballroom. (The hotel was located just down the street from Lady Bird Johnson's famous television station. Farther down that street was the beautiful Governor's Mansion, and the street ended near the State Capitol.)

The greatest test of my counseling skills was that many people usually wanted to come by our apartment in the afternoons, at the close of their business day . . . or, if they were from the school system, a little earlier, right after they finished teaching. At certain times of the year, that presented a problem, since the University's very loud, football-stadium-oriented, marching music ensemble—the widely revered Texas Longhorn Band—would be entering into its nearby afternoon practice sessions for upcoming games. The standard piece they practiced over and over was "The Eyes of Texas Are Upon You." I called it their "Texas hymn."

Just about the time I finished a counseling session with someone and we started to relax and use a few affirmations, we were likely to get drowned out by that Longhorn Band. It literally horned in on our counseling sessions.

Typically, wanting to see the brightest side of everything, I often said to my counselees, "Oh, don't mind them. They are just cheering us on." But who knows? Maybe that stirring marching music really did make a contribution to my counselees' well-being. In fact, I always felt the Longhorn Band of the University of Texas helped launch my counseling ministry, whether anybody intended such a thing or not—and certainly regardless of whether *I* meant for it to do so.

For two and a half years, things moved along smoothly. Kelly went to and from the University; Richard went to and from school; and I conducted my pioneer ministry at home and at the hotel. Life was good and getting better all the time, I reflected.

AN UNEXPECTED EVENT

Suddenly my "shining moment" took a difficult and unexpected turn. One day Kelly did not come home from the University as expected. A call finally came from his office saying, "Your husband is at the hospital." That, along with the name of the hospital, is all I was told.

The chairman of our Board, a longtime friend of Kelly's, got the same message. He telephoned me moments later while I was sitting in a daze trying to pull myself together. He said, "Wait for me. I'll drive you over there."

We arrived within minutes and were ushered into a private room. A hospital worker came in, took my hands, and said, "I'm sorry, Mrs. Ponder. It was a heart attack. Your husband was stricken just outside the English Building at the University. By the time the ambulance got him to the hospital. . . ." The hospital worker paused to collect his thoughts, then began again. "I'm sorry to inform you that your husband has died from a heart attack."

I was stunned beyond my ability to understand. Immobilized.

In a state of numbness and shock, I asked, "May I see the body?"

The hospital worker led me to the gurney on which Kelly had arrived. I looked at my husband through a haze of gathering grief, made the requested identification, then said to our Board chairman, "He is not here."

Even in my distress and pain, I realized that Kelly Ponder's wonderful, vivacious spirit was gone. Only the shell was left behind.

His longtime friend, the Chairman, quietly drove me home. During the drive, he finally said, "We need to do some thinking and planning."

First, he drove to Austin High School and picked up Richard, whom I had already telephoned with the tragic news, asking that he meet the Chairman outside. Then the Chairman telephoned the Ponder family and talked with my sister-in-law, informing her of what had happened. Next, he raised the matter of a funeral, suggesting that we get in touch with the Unity minister in Fort Worth and ask that she conduct it. She and her husband had been especially good friends of Kelly's and mine. They agreed to drive down to conduct an 11 A.M. service, two days hence.

The following day, our apartment was filled with people who attended Unity of Austin, as well as University staff members who had worked with Kelly. Dr. Haskew, Vice-Chancellor of the University, and Dr. Boatwright, chairman of Kelly's department, came by to express their condolences.

I was numb but grateful for the thoughtfulness those wonderful people expressed, and for the food that arrived. I was in no mood for eating, but my son and his friends were. I did send some to the grieving Ponder family, who were staying at a nearby motel.

I had my first integrated Unity group in Austin, and members of the black community sent me red roses with a card that said simply, "Your South Austin friends love you." At the same time as the Austin funeral, a memorial service was held at Unity Church of Birmingham, where Kelly had grown up. Meanwhile, students from Kelly's University classes attended the Austin funeral, along with University staff and members of Unity of Austin. It was a crowded event. Some of Richard's teenage friends said, "We've never seen so many cute girls at a funeral before."

NOW WHAT?

My grieving congregation expected me to take several weeks off before returning to the lecture platform. But I realized that would only delay the period of intense mourning that I—and all of us—were experiencing. After considering everything deeply, I felt the wisest course to take, hard though it might be, was to go ahead with the next Sunday's lecture—after his funeral the previous Wednesday. The sooner we all faced together what had happened, the sooner the healing could begin.

With tears in my eyes and voice, I gave the following Sunday's lecture, titling it "They Shall Be Comforted." We all cried together as we moved through the service. The thought I shared that seemed most comforting to everyone was this: "When sudden death occurs, it means the person has just been touched by an angel."

We all went through a period of inner searching over Kelly's premature death. Some of my congregants, not meaning to be cruel, still said bluntly, "If what you teach is true, why did this happen? Why did you lose a wonderful husband in the prime of his life, when you both seemed so right together?"

My only response was, "Ask God. I don't have the answer."

BITTER AND SWEET

Some of the most hurtful words anyone said to me about that intense period of grief and mourning came much later: "You never really cried again over Kelly's death."

I was stunned over that remark. While ministers in those days were often taught that grief and other difficult emotions were "not spiritual," my response to his death was based on what I felt was best for everyone, including myself. I told that person, "I cried for five years over his death, but in private. Richard was still at home and witnessed it. And I have cried in my heart ever since."

My memories of him reflect now on the kind, thoughtful little deeds he constantly performed for me, unasked and unexpected. I recall the sheer sweetness of the man—the companionable way I could talk to him about anything or nothing, the way he loved to stay home and just be with me, the manner in which he insisted on helping me with my work when he had a full workload of his own.

Frequently, he even made the morning coffee and brought it to my bedside. Even though that may have been a gentle hint for me to "rise and shine," I had never before experienced such courtesies, kindnesses, and considerate ways—nor have I since. Perhaps those kinds of unique people are rationed out carefully—one to a lifetime. To say he was "the great love of my life" would be putting it mildly.

One friend who had known me since early adulthood may have summarized it best, if rather bluntly, when she said, "Kelly must have married you for love. He certainly didn't marry you for money—because in those days you didn't have any."

A satisfying thought.

IN TRIBUTE

As the time went slowly by, I asked myself the same kinds of questions many people had asked. "Do I really believe what I'm teaching? That all things work together for good? If so, why did this happen . . . when I'd tried so hard for so long and finally seemed to be reaping professional and personal benefits from my efforts?"

I had no answer then either.

"Should I go on or should I call it quits?"

No answer.

Since I had a pioneer ministry that was not yet paying its own way, Unity School was willing to place me in an established church so I could get back on my feet emotionally without having to deal simultaneously with the pains of a growing church. But I declined their offer. In tribute to Kelly, I wanted to carry through and complete his dream of establishing Unity in the capital city of Texas. When I talked with Richard, he said, "Let's stay and see this through." He loved Austin. With all of its sports activities and wonderful year-around weather, it was the perfect place for a teenager to grow up. So we decided that "rise or fall," we'd remain. Also, my Unity of Austin members let me know they were anxious that I not leave. They had lost Kelly. They did not feel they could deal with losing me, too.

What the congregation did not know was that I used Kelly's insurance money—scant though it was—to help keep our young ministry afloat financially while I continued to teach prosperity laws and slowly develop our overall prosperity consciousness. No one but my son and I ever knew of our—and Kelly's—contribution after he was gone, the ultimate sacrifice.

Kelly had, however, looked ahead to the end of my ministry in Austin. His own plans had been to complete that year of work at the University of Texas, then teach at a college in Florida. When that time came, he wanted me to give up church work and continue to write only if I wished.

"You don't need to write any more on prosperity," he said. "You've already done it."

Only years later did I realize that had he lived, my "special and different" mission in life might never have been fulfilled in the immensely satisfying way it finally was.

But what a price to pay!

A MEMORABLE ANNIVERSARY GIFT

Over two decades later, on the twenty-fifth anniversary of our wedding, my life had changed dramatically, yet still I wondered if Kelly—wherever he was—would remember that special anniversary. For him to do so would not have been unprecedented, since occasionally over the years, in connection with various outstanding events, he had communicated with me in dreams.

The night of our twenty-fifth wedding anniversary, I had—not a dream, but a "visitation" from him that was much more vivid than a dream.

I found myself walking in a flower-filled hillside garden when I spied Kelly across the way.

Excitedly, I rushed over to him, calling, "Kelly! Kelly! Kelly!" Before he could respond, I began quickly recounting my various accomplishments over the previous twenty-five years.

To each one he quietly replied, "I know."

When I finally stopped to take a deep breath, he said sadly, "I wish I could stay"—and he was gone.

Much later, when I was visiting a long-time, trusted friend who had experienced both triumphs and tragedies of the heart, I hesitantly described Kelly's special anniversary gift to me—those five words, "I wish I could stay."

My friend listened compassionately. After a long silence, his eyes filled with tears as he finally said, "What a love story!"

CHAPTER 9

That Special Saga Continues

Ironically, Kelly's death was the beginning of a whole new era for me.

A few months later, a retired military couple began attending my lectures and helping me at our meetings. Then a lawyer from San Antonio, eighty miles away, started driving regularly to my classes and services. He and his wife also cheered me on. These two couples came to be among my best helpers and friends, just when I needed them most. My longtime church workers also blessed me in countless ways.

As Unity of Austin gradually prospered, some large, lump-sum tithe offerings made it possible for us to lease offices in the posh Westgate building, overlooking the State Capitol. We called it "Unity at the Westgate"—another milestone.

In their elegant top-floor restaurant (where, in the rarefied ambience, the Governor and other state officials regularly lunched), I often entertained visiting speakers, and I held Board meetings in an adjacent private room—also atop the Westgate. In addition, I entertained guests in the private club on the same floor. From there, we enjoyed a unique view of the lighted University tower in one direction and the State Capitol, impressive with its nighttime lighting, in another direction.

In the mid-sixties, Richard went into the military. At about the same time, I began to write one book a year, and because of the many speaking invitations I was receiving, I decided to take my show on the road. "Have Books, Will Travel" became my theme. As I did this research, writing, and traveling, I still mourned not only Kelly's death, but that of my first husband as well. All of the hurtful emotion I had been unable to release so long ago with my first husband's death now came pouring out. The double shock of two deaths hit me all at once, and I began to release—though privately—the grief from those two brief marriages. It became a much-needed emotional cleansing process, which cleared the way for a new life to begin.

However—while I had lost a Ponder husband, I gained a Ponder family. My sister-in-law and mother-in-law insisted that I spend all holidays with them when I was not working. They were a great comfort to me and became "my Texas family." Since they now lived in Dallas, once I began my nationwide lecture ministry, their home was a convenient stopping-off place to rest and recuperate after my travels. When Kelly proposed, he'd thrown in his sister's good Southern cooking as an incentive. That part of his proposal was something I enjoyed for years to come.

A NEW LIFE DEVELOPS

Toward the end of the 1960s, I began to get that divine restlessness again and to feel as though my work of pioneering Unity in Austin was complete. Someone else could take that ministry and proceed with it. And if that happened, what was I to do?

The fact I did not yet realize was that for some time, as the well-known affirmation states, "SPIRIT HAS A

DIVINE PLAN FOR THE NEXT STEP IN MY LIFE."[13] The attorney from San Antonio, who finally wore out two Lincoln automobiles driving back and forth between Austin and San Antonio for my classes and services, was not there by accident.

By the late 1960s, he had said to me on several occasions, "You've done what you can do for Unity in Austin. You have gotten this group launched. Now it's time to move on. Come to San Antonio, where you are needed for further pioneering work."

In the spring of 1969, the elderly minister who at one time had a large, successful ministry in San Antonio passed on at the age of 90—"with her boots on." That, of course, freed a new minister to go in and revive the Unity work there.

Meanwhile, my dear mother-in-law, the senior Mrs. Ponder, had been saying to me, "Catherine, you've mourned over my son long enough. It's time you got on with your life."

I said, "Mother, it's not that simple," and left it at that—though I appreciated her usual gracious consideration.

The lawyer from San Antonio contacted the Association of Unity Churches[14] and requested that I be allowed to give a series of lectures in San Antonio, to determine if the people in that area were receptive to me and to having a full-time Unity ministry again. When the Association agreed, he went out into the highways and byways to gather together people of like

---

13. For more information on the Divine Plan, see *Open Your Mind to Prosperity*, by Catherine Ponder (1971, DeVorss & Co., Marina del Rey, CA 90294), chapter 7.

14. The Unity ministries pioneered by the author have all been affiliated with the Association of Unity Churches (P.O. Box 610, Lee's Summit, MO, 64063, USA).

mind to launch a revived Unity in San Antonio. He made all the arrangements, including finding a meeting place and contacting everyone—near and far, in and around San Antonio—who had previously shown an interest in our inspirational teachings.

COMING HOME

And so one Sunday in San Antonio, despite the rain that was pouring down, 300 enthusiastic people showed up for my first talk. When I walked out on the platform, before I even spoke, they gave me a standing ovation. It was like coming home.

Afterward, when I greeted them individually, each one had a story to tell me: either they had heard me lecture elsewhere, attended a prosperity seminar I conducted somewhere in the United States, read my articles in the Unity publications, read some of my early books, or had a friend or relative who'd heard me or read me. Or they had connected with Unity through other means, such as the world-famous Silent Unity Prayer Department (to whom many of them had written with gratifying results) or the former "Unity Viewpoint" radio program (that was broadcast in San Antonio from Unity School for many years). I was not new to these people, nor were they new to me. They already knew me inwardly, and I felt I knew them. It was more like a reunion than a beginning.

As I continued with my lecture series there, the attorney and I soon realized that he was right. Not only was my work in Austin finished—but also my work in the famed Alamo City of Texas was just beginning.

And what a happy beginning it was. Of the several ministries I'd had, this group was by far the most friendly and outgoing. San Antonio proved to be more than simply a historic tourist attraction where every day was "fiesta time." It had a light-hearted party atmosphere that gave everything and everybody a lift. I could feel the long mourning period I had experienced in Austin coming to a close.

FIESTA TIME BEGINS FOR ME

Then a friend wrote me what I considered to be a strange message. She said, "You are going to meet someone who is very different. You will tend to overlook him and to discount his many abilities and accomplishments. But I *implore* you to give him a chance. There's more to him than meets the eye. He could have a great influence for good on your life."

I dismissed it all as nonsense.

Until it happened.

A doctor of chiropractic who was somewhere near my age began attending Sunday services—alone. Known by his patients and friends as "Dr. Bill," he told me he was there because he heard I'd come to town. He knew I'd lectured for a number of chiropractic conventions, including the Parker Seminars in the Fort Worth/Dallas area. Many of his friends, also chiropractors, had heard me speak and met me personally. He, himself, had read my books, and now he wanted to hear me speak in person.

I was very familiar with chiropractic work, and had been for years. Our family was introduced to the power of chiropractic when my father began experiencing violent, recurring headaches that no type of treatment alleviated—until he got his first chiropractic adjustment. That was the end of his violent headaches. I myself had begun getting chiropractic treatments while

I was in Austin, at the beginning of my nationwide lecture/seminar work and the extensive air and ground travel it required. And as I continued that work from San Antonio, I spent a lot of time stuck in particular physical positions, such as standing while I lectured and sitting for extended periods while I was on long flights.

I was looking for a San Antonio chiropractor for ongoing treatment between those long trips. Several had attended my Sunday talks, but none were located on my side of town, so I didn't seek them out. But when this man continued attending my church and even began regular tithing, I said to myself, "He means business in his inspirational studies." Since he was also conveniently located on my side of town, I eventually called his office for an appointment.

On a bright spring day I arrived for treatment. He gave me an excellent adjustment, and when he finished he said, "I'd like to see you in my office before you go."

When I sat down in his office, I asked, "Doctor, is something wrong?"

"Yes," he replied. "When I attended your first Sunday service, the moment you began speaking, an electric shock went through me. I have been wanting to have lunch with you ever since, but I've been unable to get your unlisted telephone number. I didn't want to ask anyone at church, because I didn't want to cause gossip. But when you finally called my office for an appointment, I vowed I'd take up the matter with you in person. Will you have dinner with me?" His desk-side manner was a little overwhelming, and totally unexpected.

When I caught my breath, I said, "When did you have in mind?"

"Tonight."

"I'm booked for the next ten days." I whipped out my appointment book, which I had to carry in my pocketbook to keep my complex local and long-distance schedule straight. I tipped the book toward him, as though that would have allowed him to confirm with his own eyes the truth of what I'd just said. "You can see for yourself all the appointments and trips I am committed to for the time being."

He impatiently agreed to wait, but now he had my telephone number as part of the personal information I so trustingly supplied to him by filling out his forms. He asked if he might telephone me in the meantime. Innocently enough, and still surprised at his boldness, I agreed that he could.

He did several times, and sent roses as well.

He did not realize that I also wanted time to have him checked out. My attorney friend used whatever methods attorneys use to do such things and later reported back, "He has a good record. Don't hesitate to accept his invitations."

We had been told in Ministerial School never to go out with our parishioners, and to keep our spiritual work and personal lives separate. When I brought this up with him, he said, "I am not one of your parishioners. I am not attending because of Unity. I am attending because of you. If anyone else were the minister, I would not come."

I wasn't exactly sure his logic was airtight, but his response somehow seemed reasonable, and it did make me feel easier about seeing him socially.

FIESTA TIME CONTINUES

Dr. Bill was short in stature, and had blue eyes and light-colored, slightly graying hair. He certainly was not the type of person I was used to seeing on a personal basis. But with his distinct personality, he was unfazed by my initial reluctance and was unstoppable. On our first dinner date, he took me to one of the most historic restaurants in San Antonio, the Grey Moss Inn. (It's a landmark there even today, many years later.) It was situated in a rustic setting, and the chef cooked outside on a smoked grill. The inside was filled with candlelight and wildflowers—all unforgettable.

After that first night, he insisted on taking me to lunch, dinner, the theater, the movies, and arts-and-crafts shows. He delighted in pointing out the historic sights of San Antonio, such as the famed Alamo, the other five picturesque missions, and the downtown River Walk, helping me become acquainted with the city and with how to get around in it. His next project was to acquaint me with the beautiful Hill Country north of San Antonio. Later still, he introduced me to Mexico, through the border towns located south of San Antonio. This man, in fact, gradually opened a whole new world to me. He would put me on airplanes for my out-of-state lecture trips, then meet my planes in the middle of the night when I returned. He later claimed he had to court me at the airport if he wanted to see me at all. The man's persistence exceeded that of anyone I'd ever known.

Suddenly I remembered that strange message my friend had sent me before I met him. *So this is what she meant,* I thought. A new man who took me to raise, whether I meant for him to or not. She was right. Dr. Bill was different and I would not have taken him seriously—except that he never gave me a chance to do otherwise.

What I admired most about him was that he was a self-made man. He had used his GI bill for a portion of his basic education after coming out of World War II, then worked his way through Texas Chiropractic College. He also did graduate work at the National Chiropractic College in Chicago. He loved the great state of Texas and noted that he happened to be a Texan who had the misfortune of being born elsewhere.

"I wasn't born in Texas," he often said, "but I got here as fast as I could."

TONIC TIME

From the start, I never had a chance. This man had my number.

He was soon talking marriage. He didn't ask me. He told me, though indirectly.

"*When* we get married. . . ," he once said casually, at the beginning of a statement about something else.

I gasped, interrupting. "When we *what?*"

He ignored my dismay and continued talking, as if I'd not said anything. And he continued with his "when we get married" theme.

I thought, "Well, at least he knows what he wants. He doesn't have to go off and 'pray about it' like Kelly Ponder did."

I couldn't help but be impressed by his self-confidence. I knew he had been married previously, but many years before.

What was I to do? My lawyer friend's wife said bluntly, "Marry him. Together you can build a whole new life, which you need. You've both had some hard knocks in the past. This could make up for everything."

And so it did. We were married in the home of that attorney and his wife. The new Unity minister from Austin drove over and performed the ceremony. The occasion was not so much exciting as it was pleasant and satisfying. He simply seemed like a member of the family, very comfortable to be with, and it all felt right. He had a bright mind and a quick wit, which balanced my much quieter, more serious way of viewing life. He could see the funny side of everything and had a quip for every occasion. (When he wanted to tease me, he would call me "The Pope-ette.") He was like a tonic for me.

We had kept our courtship quiet. No one from the church knew anything about it or the wedding. We planned things that way, since we wanted no speculation or talk about these personal matters. But everyone was overjoyed when I revealed to them that the marriage had taken place. They assumed it meant I was in San Antonio to stay.

NO PLACE LIKE HOME

Before leaving Austin, I got rid of all the furniture and household goods that might remind me of Kelly Ponder. I had gone to San Antonio determined to put the past behind me, and I moved into a brand-new furnished apartment.

Now, my husband began talking to me about our purchasing a home, emphasizing the privacy it would bring as well as its investment value. Prior to our marriage, we agreed that he would have the last word on cars and I would have the last word on houses—and I wasn't yet convinced. I kept saying, "I don't have time to keep house, nor do I even know how to. I've always had to work."

"I'll take care of overseeing the house and yard," he said. "We'll eat out some, order in some, and I'll use a grill for most of our at-home cooking."

It took him a year and a half to convince me, but I finally consented to his accompanying a realtor, who was also a patient of his, to begin checking out properties. I specified that the house must be in a certain price range, with a mortgage no more than a certain amount. None of this fazed him. He launched his search with my specifications in hand.

For months, every time he thought he might have found the perfect house, I looked and said, "No, this isn't it." I wasn't being overly fussy or attempting to obstruct what he was doing. I simply knew what I wanted—and hadn't yet seen it.

Meanwhile, he was owed $10,000 from a mortgage he had been carrying, related to a business deal he made prior to our marriage. He kept saying, "If only I had that $10,000! It would help with the house purchase."

I kept responding, "Release it and leave it alone. We can make it with or without that money."

But he wanted to do his part.

One day he called excitedly from his office and said, "You were right. When I released it, everything changed. The people involved now want to pay off that mortgage. They're putting a check for $10,000 in the mail."

When the check arrived, he proudly handed it to me to deposit. That was my spiritual sign that our house was near.

A few days later, my husband phoned me excitedly and said, "I think the realtor and I finally found the house! It's in the right price range and we can get a mortgage for the amount you wanted. You must see it at once! Furthermore, the realtor gave me a key, so you can see it when no one else is around to distract you."

It was a brand-new, well-decorated little house in the Inspiration Hills section of San Antonio, with just the right shade of carpet already installed and a beautiful decorator's touch everywhere. Now, finally, in my early forties, I was going to have my own home, thanks to a caring husband. Knowing that helped to blot out so much hurt and disappointment from the past.

AN UNEXPECTED ENCOUNTER

One day soon after we moved into our new house, I was presenting a prosperity seminar in Houston when I received an unexpected call at my hotel. The telephone operator said, "The actress and singer Giselle MacKenzie has been trying to reach you. Here's her number." I knew her name well. I remembered having seen her accompany Jack Benny on the violin on television, and I'd heard her sing on the popular "Your Hit Parade" radio program.

When I returned her call, she told me she was one of my readers and that she was currently appearing in a prominent Houston hotel. She said she'd hoped to meet me on this Texas trip, and had been amazed to read in the newspaper that I was also in Houston! She told me that the night before, as she went to sleep, she was saying to herself, "Tomorrow I am going to make contact with Catherine Ponder"—though she didn't know exactly how that would happen.

When I returned her call, she also invited me to have lunch with her and her manager. When we met, she related to me story after story of how she had used ideas from my book *The Dynamic Laws of Prosperity* to help herself and a number of struggling actors. She invited me and my party to attend her last performance in their largest ballroom that night. Although it was sold out, she arranged to have the waiters clear the table where water glasses and other supplies were kept, in order to create seating for me and several friends.

I purposely finished my seminar a bit early, then my friends and I raced across town to be on hand for her show. Her performance was delightful, and the mayor presented her with a bouquet of red roses in appreciation for her visit to Houston.

Earlier, she had invited me to come backstage to her dressing room after the show. When I did, she presented me with those roses, since she was departing the next morning by plane for California. Thus, I went back to my new San Antonio house and "christened" it with Giselle's red roses—a nice celebrity touch for my very first home!

REAPPEARANCE OF AN OLD FEELING

My years in beautiful San Antonio were such busy ones. Adding to my own full schedule of church work and lectures, my husband and I joined two country clubs and one private city club downtown. These we enjoyed personally and in private, away from our work, though a couple of times a year we entertained several dozen church workers at one of our country clubs, in appreciation for their volunteerism. After our house was finally furnished—piece by piece with custom-made furniture from Mexico—we held parties for our church workers there, too, crowding them all in.

During that era, numerous out-of-town guest speakers for the church came to San Antonio at our invitation, and we entertained many of them at either our clubs or our home. It was all stimulating and exciting, but I finally realized that with the comings and goings of so many visiting speakers as well as my continuing nationwide lecture work and the ongoing development of a happy, successful new ministry, I was getting no writing done—and writing was my greatest outreach. I felt strongly that "my song would not be sung" until I had written a number of other books—all of which were awaiting my attention.

This realization brought back that old divine restlessness, which I could not subdue. How could I continue with a buzzing local ministry, travel to seminars, deal with a new marriage, and still find time to write books? In addition to handling his own work, my husband helped me in every way. But I realized that sooner or later I'd have to make a decision that would inevitably lead to major changes.

It came sooner.

For a while, the restless feeling faded into the background and I continued being very happy in my San Antonio ministry. But after several years in San Antonio, whenever I traveled west and conducted seminars in Southern California, the restlessness returned with full force. To all appearances, I was developing a behavioral pattern of "create, then let go"—which sometimes I, and perhaps others as well, interpreted as an inability or an unwillingness to dig in permanently. But always I knew "Spirit had a plan," and my moving from place to place was only *one* part of it.

CHAPTER 10

Hollywood On The Desert

I was introduced to California's famous Palm Springs area by a Countess.

On that occasion in the mid-1960s, I was visiting Southern California for the first time—as a Field Lecturer for Unity School, conducting prosperity lectures there for various churches. When Countess Viola Lukawiecki, an old friend, invited me to her home in the desert, she said, "You haven't seen the best of Southern California until you visit Palm Springs."

We drove there after I presented a late-evening lecture nearby, arriving in the middle of the night. As we came into the town, I was intrigued to see streetlights attached to the palm trees. They served as the only night-lighting on Palm Canyon Drive, the main street. Then the next morning, when I looked out the window of her guest room, I saw the most beautiful mountain I'd ever seen—all in pink. During the day it constantly changed color, until by evening it was a vivid lavender, then purple. Suddenly I knew what the songwriter must have meant by "purple mountain majesties." Had she found Palm Springs, too?

And so began my love affair with an area that intrigued me before and has continued to intrigue me—and lots of other people—ever since.

THE COUNTESS

Southern-born, Viola had been in the American Armed Forces in Europe during World War II, where she married a high-ranking military officer. After the war and his death, she remained in Europe with friends. Then, in romantic, historic Vienna, she was introduced to a Polish Count who had survived internment in a concentration camp, though his properties and assets had been confiscated.

Slight of build but tall, impressive, and with the look of aristocracy, he fell in love with Viola. Beautiful she was not, but her extraordinary charm is what people noticed when they were around her, so she was regarded as beautiful anyway.

They were married in that exotic Austrian setting and soon came to the United States. I first met them while Viola, accompanied by the Count, and I were studying at Unity School. Later, because of the Count's health, they were advised to settle in Southern California. A few years after they made that move, he died suddenly. Viola chose to remain there, to pioneer Unity in Palm Springs.

During my brief stay with her, she showed me all the attractions—from Palm Springs itself to Palm Desert, about fifteen miles away. Personally seeing the luxurious homes and lavish lifestyles of so many well-known show-business personalities caused me to understand why the area was often called "Hollywood on the Desert." I told Viola that if the time ever came when I could concentrate more fully on my writing, I would love to live in the area. She encouraged me to make the move, noting that many well-known writers had found that the quietness and beauty of the area made it a perfect place to work. Among them were Erle Stanley Gardner, who authored the renowned "Perry Mason" detective novels and inspired the long-running television series of the same name. Others who were later to gain immense popularity as novelists while writing in the desert included Sidney Shelton, Harold Robbins, and Joseph Waumbaugh, famed for his gritty tales of the Los Angeles Police Department.

For almost ten years thereafter, I received notes, cards, and pictures of the area from Viola, all of which included variations on this theme: "*When* you come to Palm Springs to live, you must become a member of the Racquet Club. You must also join a country club. And you must live in the posh Las Palmas neighborhood of Palm Springs." She kept describing the lifestyle she felt I should have there in the desert—one that she herself, as a consequence of business and social connections, had fully embraced.

I thought, "That's all wonderful, but how could I ever arrange it?" At that point, I never really imagined it could happen.

HOW A PREDICTION CAME TRUE

By the early 1970s, however, after establishing Unity Church of San Antonio, I was flooded by that familiar divine discontent every time I lectured in Southern California. Often at the conclusion of my work there, I took an extra day and quietly went to Palm Springs to study it and further check it out. My feelings were always the same. "*This is it.*" So my longing for it and my excitement at the prospect of living there mounted.

"Picture a thing and bring it through, rather than trying to reason it through or force it through. You can hasten your good by picturing it." That valuable suggestion was part of every book I wrote and every lecture

I presented. Now, as my restlessness increased, I was ready to take my own advice in regard to living where I wanted to live. I made a wheel-of-fortune prayer-map, picturing life in Palm Springs.

Finally, in the spring of 1973, I was scheduled to conduct a number of Prosperity Seminars in Southern California. They were spaced a month apart. That gave me time to visit Palm Springs at the conclusion of each one—which I did. Countess Viola had retired and left the area by then, but I had begun to feel quite comfortable there on my own.

After my 1973 New Year's service in San Antonio, Dr. Bill and I flew to Palm Springs so he could see the area. Though he routinely lauded San Antonio as his Promised Land, he was willing to take a look at Palm Springs. I had, in fact, informed him before our marriage of my desire to live there someday, and he'd felt he could safely agree, since he saw no possibility that the move could actually come about. But in the intervening years, our growing financial potential made it possible for us to consider such a drastic change. During that time, I realized how astute Dr. Bill was at handling money, so I asked him to become our mutual Business Manager, though we still worked together closely, discussing everything before he made a transaction. As a result of this collaboration, and because of the continuing, spreading success of my books, new horizons began opening up for us. I was often reminded of a well-known success axiom: *Two agreed tune in on a Third Power.*

Also, after so many years in pastoral ministry, I felt the time had arrived for me to honor my readers worldwide, who were regularly demanding more attention. Tithes from those readers had helped found Unity of Austin and Unity Church of San Antonio. What seemed fair was that I now found a global work[15] in appreciation for their continued financial support and interest, and in order to serve them better.

With all this in mind, when Dr. Bill and I visited the Palm Springs area for a few days together after that New Year's service, he said with a twinkle in his eyes, "I've always loved Texas and felt I'd spend the rest of my life there, but I can see why you're so intrigued with this town. It's a mecca—not only for the rich and famous, but also for working people like us. I feel we could be very happy living here."

During subsequent spring trips, everything fell into place: we were able to find ministry space in nearby Palm Desert, which was a dusty little desert town at the time. (That area had reportedly been occupied by General Patton and his troops during World War II, when he was planning his North African offensive. The terrain was similar to that of the future battleground.) We also located a "fixer-upper" house in the Old Movie Colony neighborhood of Palm Springs—which did take us several years to fix up. Later, it proved to be a great investment, as real estate prices climbed in Southern California.

The Association of Unity Churches provided a new minister for Unity in San Antonio; my husband retired from his practice; our new house in San Antonio and his office building there quickly sold. By August 1, 1973, we had arrived in Palm Springs to live out my dream of almost ten years' standing.

---

15.   For information, please write Unity Worldwide, P.O. Drawer 1278, Palm Desert, CA 92261, USA.

LIFE—PALM SPRINGS STYLE

And what a dream it turned out to be! All the things the Countess had written me about, saying they *should* happen, did. The world-famous Racquet Club, for instance. The handsome Charles Farrell, a long-time movie and television star, had long since sold the Racquet Club but still managed it. He was greatly revered, not only by the Hollywood community, but also in Palm Springs, having served as one of its early mayors. However, since we were not from Hollywood, our becoming members of the Racquet Club seemed impossible. Our lawyer, doctor, accountant, banker, and insurance agent all assured us that "it couldn't be done."

Again, I pictured it: our being welcomed into the Racquet Club. Getting there took a year, during which we seemed to stumble upon just the right people to sponsor our membership. When my husband announced to everyone who had said membership was impossible that we were now members, they were stunned.

Countess Viola's dream that we should join a country club came true for us more easily. Bermuda Dunes Country Club, home of the annual Bob Hope Desert Golf Classic, was the only club in the desert at the time that had a twenty-seven-hole golf course. Its clubhouse was located atop a hill, overlooking golf courses on several sides. Such famous personalities as Clark Gable and Fred Waring had been among its members; titans of business and "old money," now retired, crowded its membership list. Bermuda Dunes welcomed us! My husband quietly observed, "We are knee-deep in millionaires."

My work schedule—which included not just writing but also helping Dr. Bill set up our global ministry—kept me happily busy most of the time at my desk. And because his work schedule allowed it, he often had lunch at that club, not far from our Palm Desert head-quarters. This allowed him a unique opportunity to create and nurture numerous social relationships that benefited us both—relationships that I simply would not have had the time to keep up with. He met, became friends with, and heard many an impressive story from fellow members. In fact, he dived into the desert lifestyle as though he had been born to the manor, loving every minute of it.

We also became members of the Palm Springs Tennis Club, which was owned at the time by a couple from Chicago who were prominent there in business. The wife was an artist, and she used her artistic skills freely to decorate the club for every holiday occasion. Whereas the more conservative Racquet Club was not inclined to do so, she constantly added colorful, festive touches to seasonal parties and gatherings at her Club. It was a fun place to take our many guests, who, out of curiosity, found numerous reasons to visit us in Palm Springs in the early years. My husband was delighted to show them around. He was much more the "party animal" than I, although I tried to cooperate with his outgoing personality and its social demands.

ENTERTAINING—PALM SPRINGS STYLE

Since we often saw famous Hollywood faces of the past and present at the Racquet Club, we tended to take out-of-state guests there, too. We once entertained a Texas oilman and his wife who'd been around the world and thought they'd seen everything—until they got to the Racquet Club. There, we practically had to hold them down to keep them from going into hysterics over all the well-known Hollywood personalities surrounding us at other tables.

On our way out of the club with that couple, we encountered a man who was awaiting his limo. The oil-man almost went nuts—again—when he saw the huge diamond ring that unknown man was casually wearing on his little finger. The four of us never could agree on just how many carats that ring must have contained, though the Texan contemplated its probable value in terms of how many oil wells would be required to purchase its equivalent. That previously conservative Texan had just "gone Hollywood" on us. He simply wanted one of those rings! Soon he was on his way back to Texas . . . to drill more oil wells.

Another time, we entertained my publisher and his wife. We purposely elected to sit in the Garden Room, where again we were in the company of countless internationally famous show-business personalities, most of whom at this time were on the dance floor. My awestruck publisher said, "This is a better show than I'd get in Las Vegas!"

On another occasion, two of my friends from Kansas City were visiting. These were very successful, well-traveled women. When we all arrived at the Bermuda Dunes Country Club for lunch, we spied a long black limousine, with a smaller black car parked just behind it.

My husband observed casually, "Former President Ford must be here playing golf—probably with Bob Hope."

When we inquired during lunch, we were told that the ex-president and the legendary comedian were, indeed, on the back nine. My world-traveled friends got so excited that they could hardly finish their lunch. Afterward, we drove along the perimeter of the golf course. There in the distance we saw President Ford and Bob Hope on the greens, surrounded by Secret

Service agents stationed in golf carts. What a way to have to play golf! But the famous players seemed to be oblivious to the obvious, and were enjoying themselves anyway—though perhaps not as much as our guests from Kansas City.

GOING GLOBAL

In spite of the "celebrity-itis" of the Palm Springs area, I began all over again to get the feeling I once had in wartime Washington. I knew I needed time to follow my own "special and different" drummer and to accomplish what it demanded.

I worked at home in Palm Springs, in my writing studio. Every weekday morning after my husband and I declared prosperity affirmations together, he left to work with my staff at the ministry headquarters in Palm Desert, where mail arrived regularly from around the world. Sometimes, so did my readers—unannounced.

Soon after we brought my global ministry to Palm Desert, that previously quiet little area was incorporated. (How quiet had it been? So quiet that one of its major annual events was the fall season's "golf-cart parade," which, according to reports, was regarded by the populace as compelling entertainment.) After the incorporation, it quickly became a boom town, beautifully planned and built, with palm trees and both winter and summer flowers in profusion everywhere.

My global readership was delighted that I now had a ministry just for them. And they responded with great interest and appreciation. Two readers sent in checks of $1000 each to inaugurate our building fund. In each of my prior church ministries, we called such accounts "The Gold Dust Building Fund," which was taken from a concept in *The Dynamic Laws of Prosperity*, and it had caught on. People responded, and each of those churches later got its own building.

In 1980, thanks to donors to The Gold Dust Building Fund, we were able to buy the old Hopalong Cassidy building, located on the main street in Palm Desert, and gradually remodel it to meet our global needs. The structure was originally built by William Boyd, who portrayed the heroic, clean-living Cassidy in over five dozen movies during the 1930s and 1940s, and in the television series that followed. Boyd later invested heavily in Palm Desert real estate. He was a friend of Gene Autry, Roy Rogers, and other Western stars of that era.

In our global work from that building, we were able to function more efficiently and comfortably, and also to modernize various aspects of our operation. This included computerizing certain phases of the ministry's outreach, which simplified the schedule of our staff, as well as better serving my readers.

WORK AND PLAY

Meanwhile, I started writing my "Millionaires of the Bible" series from my Palm Springs study. Beginning with *The Millionaires of Genesis,* I wrote a book a year for the next several years, until some of my older books demanded revision, which took me away from further work on those Biblical millionaires. Now, as the twenty-first century gets underway, I plan to return to my book-a-year schedule as soon as other matters allow me to do so.

My health-conscious husband, knowing the intensity of my working routine, always insisted after each book was completed that we take a short vacation. This was in the era when only the affluent cruised—prior to the time when multiple, low-cost cruise lines appeared and their ships became a popular way for the masses to vacation. But I never adjusted to cruises. I appreciated the beautiful surroundings, the stimulating shipboard lifestyle, and the sightseeing trips in various ports. But all too soon I'd get "cabin fever." Since I had not yet progressed spiritually to the point of being able to walk on water, I couldn't return before the ship did, which meant I was stuck there for the duration.

In spite of my quiet resistance to cruising, I am now glad I had those experiences. Certain vivid impressions stand out, such as . . .

. . . leaving behind the heat of a Palm Springs summer to enjoy the coolness of the last cruise of the season to Alaska and its ice-filled waters, its inviting towns, and its villages.

. . . hearing our guide on that same journey describe our tour group as being from "the lower 48." I was equally amazed to discover that small boats, not cars, were the main transportation from town to town there, since the terrain made roads unbuildable and therefore nonexistent in many areas.

. . . floating into Acapulco Bay and viewing the tropical hillside terrain while having breakfast aboard ship.

. . . while everyone else onboard listened attentively to a description of the engineering feats of the Panama Canal, enjoying views of the exotic tropical growth shipside, along with looking at the freighters and boats that slowly passed by, headed in the other direction. There were vessels of every color, flag, and nationality. The friendly crews waved and chatted in many languages. It was a floating United Nations.

Perhaps the most memorable of all my cruise impressions was that of returning from Canada and arriving just prior to dawn in New York Harbor with the popular song "New York, New York" playing all over the ship. The passengers gathered on deck to view the tall, lighted Statue of Liberty, standing guard like a towering angel on one side of the ship, while we absorbed a dazzling view of Manhattan with its many glittering, night-lighted buildings on the other side. What a spectacular way to conclude my cruising experiences!

At other times, Dr. Bill and I got in our station wagon and traveled around the western United States, much of which was—and still is—uncrowded and worth seeing, both in terms of scenery and historical interest and of unique work produced by local artisans. My interest in Native American arts and crafts began developing during those travels and has continued ever since, coming about quickly and easily, since I love all types of jewelry, as well as the varied artistic creations of the Native American cultures.

Many people don't know about or appreciate the heritage of the Old West, but in many areas it remains a great undiscovered secret for travelers. Among our favorite places to visit was the Arizona Biltmore Hotel in Phoenix, a creation of Frank Lloyd Wright and some of his students. We immensely enjoyed the pink adobe Arizona Inn in Tucson, where the Rockefellers used to winter. Though farther away, Santa Fe, New Mexico, was another favorite vacation spot. We also enjoyed various of the guest ranches we discovered in, around, and between those locations.

Since we could not be away from my global work for long periods, time was a major consideration. We found that spending our vacation periods in these out-of-state areas was quicker and easier than navigating among the more crowded tourist destinations of California—and we felt it was just as rewarding.

THE STETSON

At the time Dr. Bill and I married, we agreed that when special occasions called for gift-giving, we would give each other gifts we really *wanted*—which meant: no surprises. Therefore, he informed me well ahead of time that for the first birthday he would have after our wedding, he wanted a "Stetson 100" from me.

"I know a Stetson's a hat," I said. "But what does the '100' stand for?"

"You'll see," he replied.

When we shopped for his gift, I discovered soon enough that "Stetson 100" referred to a Western hat that cost at least $100—a lot of money at the time. He tried to soften the surprise of the significant expense by carefully explaining that "Stetson 100s" were associated with men of means and influence in the West and that they therefore commanded great respect. I did not take his explanation too seriously but said nothing.

Several years later, after moving to Palm Springs, we were on a vacation and found ourselves in a unique little town in Colorado that was filled with the atmosphere of the Old West. When we went into the hotel dining room for dinner, we discovered that, according to local custom, all the men who entered threw their hats atop a wide ledge over the fireplace, built especially for the purpose of hat-holding.

When the other patrons in the dining room suddenly realized that a "Stetson 100" had appeared among the large collection of Western hats thrown there—and that we were from Palm Springs by way of Texas—they began drifting over to our table to chat, either one by one or in small groups. It was like having the entire Old West pay court to us.

One person said in awe, "The only other Stetson 100 I have seen was worn by President Lyndon Johnson."

Dr. Bill's hat commanded respect and led to assumptions by others in a way I would not have imagined had I not seen it for myself. He, as things turned out, had known exactly what he was talking about when he asked for that birthday present. But at the time he got it, I'm not sure even *he* realized that one of those famous hats would eventually make it into the White House!

THERE GOES THE NEIGHBORHOOD

As for my maverick husband, he was having the time of his life. He found all kinds of ways to keep things interesting for me. Every day he had at least one funny story to tell me about some event he'd observed or participated in personally. He seemed to have a talent for drawing such experiences to him. He also made life interesting for those around him. An example: while we were living in our first Palm Springs house, in the Old Hollywood Movie Colony, Dr. Bill woke up the neighborhood every morning as he left for the office by playing the musical horn on his sports car. Just about the time our neighbors were settling down for their afternoon naps, he returned from the office and announced his arrival by playing that musical horn again. Although I never heard of any complaints about his antics, I am sure the neighbors were glad when we finally moved out of that area and into the affluent, historic Las Palmas neighborhood of Palm Springs.

Thus we left behind the star-filled ambience of the Old Hollywood Colony area. It was where Gloria Swanson had an estate just around the corner from our home. The Al Jolson estate was nearby, and the Cary Grant estate was within walking distance. The house next door to us had reportedly been built by Randolph Scott. Although our realtor never told us so, rumor had it that our own Old Hollywood Colony house was once owned by Liberace as an investment property. Its décor certainly exuded elements of his flamboyant personality when we bought it. The whole area, in fact, was infused with Hollywood celebrity history.

HOLLYWOOD NEIGHBORS—PAST AND PRESENT

Among the Hollywood personalities living in the desert either full- or part-time when we came to town were Frank Sinatra, William Powell, Kirk Douglas, Dinah Shore, Ruby Keeler, Ginger Rogers, Jolie Gabor, Ginny Simms, Joseph Cotton, Mary Martin, Alice Faye, Phil Harris, Fred Waring, Gene Autry, George Montgomery, Loretta Young, Jane Wyman, Janet Gaynor, Martha Hyer Wallace, William Holden, Lily Pons, Lucille Ball, Hoagy Carmichael, Liberace, Red Skelton, and Randolph Scott. Among these celebrated residents was also director/producer Frank Capra, legendary as "the man who came to the desert for one night and stayed fifty years."

Three Hollywood personalities who lived in the desert had the distinction, at one time or another, of being Mayors in the area. They included Bob Hope and Bing Crosby (who had served as Honorary Mayors of Palm Springs and Palm Desert) and Sonny Bono (who was elected Mayor of Palm Springs). Sonny Bono, of course, later went on to win yet another election: to the United States Congress.

Residents got accustomed to seeing such familiar faces around town, and the famous personalities enjoyed spending time there in the desert, knowing the public would generally leave them alone and give them the privacy they desired and so richly deserved.

CELEBRITY SIGHTINGS

At various social functions my husband and I attended, we often saw the show-business elite. Dr. Bill, for example, enjoyed the renowned Bob Hope Desert Golf Classic, which he attended annually, and he often visited with various celebs from the entertainment world who were on hand to participate for charity, such as Glen Campbell and Robert Stack. Around town, I routinely saw, sometimes at startlingly close range, various stars and other famous people, many of whom frequented the Racquet Club, though any personal encounters I had with them were usually few and brief.

I once was doing some last-minute Christmas shopping in a local department store when I noticed Red Skelton browsing there. I thought no more about it until I went out to the parking lot and got in my car.

Then, seeing movement out the corner of my eye, I turned and observed the red-headed comedian standing at the back door of the store, waving at me and smiling. I looked around to see if I was imagining things, wondering who he was *really* waving at. But no, it was me.

Opening my door, I called, "Yes, Mr. Skelton?"

He replied, "Lady, you got your dress caught in your car door."

A quick glance verified the accuracy of his statement. I gathered up the folds of my dress, then smiled back at him and waved. As I closed the door again and drove off, I recalled that he was known for his kindness and courtesy—and now I realized his kindness extended even to a stranger in a parking lot. (After the incident, I remembered that his late wife had been a friend of Countess Viola, who said Mrs. Skelton was equally as generous.)

On another occasion I was in the well-known Alan Ladd Store, with its enormous selection of unusual, upscale decorator items for the fashionable home.[16] Though the well-known actor himself, for whom the store was named, had passed on, his wife still ran the establishment. She was a terrific decorator and always carried unique gift items. Again during a holiday season, I had run into the store late one afternoon to look for a special gift. Suddenly I found myself standing next to a tall, distinguished-looking man who looked familiar. But I paid no attention—until he spoke, and I instantly recognized his voice. It was the famed Liberace, accompanied by his secretary, who was taking notes on a small pad.

He said to her, pointing as he spoke, "Send that piece to the Palm Springs house. Send this piece to the Los Angeles house. And send this other piece to the Las Vegas house. Send the rest of the pieces to the warehouse."

This man so loved to shop that he needed a warehouse just for the overflow! No wonder the local merchants were so happy when he came to town from one of his other houses.

The last time I saw him was a few years later as he drove out of the parking lot of a grocery store in his station wagon, which had enormous, stylized piano keys painted prominently on the side. When he gave autographs, he always drew a picture of a piano to accom-

---

16. The Alan Ladd Store closed its doors in 2002 after many years of successful and widely-acclaimed operation.

pany his signature. And the nighttime illumination in front of his estate consisted of lights that were arranged in the form of a candelabra.

The tales of Palm Springs show-business celebrities are endless and wonderful. They will continue as long as there is a "Hollywood on the desert."

NORMAL AT LAST

In spite of all the different kinds of work and play that filled my time during those years, it was doubtless one of the more normal periods of my life.

CHAPTER 11

The Palm Springs Saga Continues

Since Palm Springs is only about a hundred miles from Los Angeles—"the City of Angels"—people don't just do a lot of traveling to and fro. Many of them also have residences in both locations. Some Southern Californians go even further. In addition to their Palm Springs and Los Angeles residences, they have homes (or condos) at the beach and in the mountains and sometimes in the San Francisco or San Diego areas as well. They enjoy them all as the seasons change. No wonder California is called "the Golden State"!

The manager of our country club in Palm Springs suggested that my husband and I consider joining the popular Los Angeles Club. He made his suggestion with our convenience in mind, thinking we might want to have somewhere special to dine when we went into that city to shop, attend the theater, or go to either personal or work-related events. So he arranged with the Manager there for us to visit and have a meal.

At the time, it was considered one of the three most prestigious clubs in Los Angeles, and when we went there, we felt it fully lived up to its reputation! Founded by J. Paul Getty for his Los Angeles employees and their business associates, it was friendly and well-appointed. Located atop the Getty-Union Bank Building on world-famous Wilshire Boulevard, it provided a wonderful view of the surrounding city, with the mountains in the background.

During our first party at the Los Angeles Club, a gathering for new members, we were invited by one of the Trustees to be her special guests at various upcoming social events. She was the Manager of an insurance company nearby and used the club for many of her company's functions. Through the long-term friendship we developed with her, we met many club members who were highly-regarded in the Los Angeles business and professional communities.

CONNECTING WITH THE CITY OF ANGELS

Only years later did I learn that she and many others we met at those parties attended the internationally known Founder's Church of Religious Science,[17] less than a mile away. Founder's Church is affiliated with the Religious Science-Science of Mind movement[18], which has always been a major seller of my books. It was established years earlier by Dr. Ernest Holmes, whose spiritual healing philosophy and network of churches gained a worldwide audience. Holmes had also been well-known on the Los Angeles social scene.

But just as I didn't know to begin with that some club members attended Founder's Church, little did any of *them* know—since they wouldn't have recognized the name I went by—that I had lectured in that very church years earlier. In social situations, I always wanted to reduce the hubbub that occasionally arose if people knew me as an author rather than simply as a

---

17. Founder's Church of Religious Science, 3281 West Sixth St., Los Angeles, CA 90020.

18. The Religious Science–Science of Mind movement, 3251 West Sixth St., Los Angeles, CA 90020.

person whose company they enjoyed. Thus, Dr. Bill and I always used my married name, which was totally unrelated to the name "Ponder." I wasn't interested in personal celebrity or in being the center of attention at parties. In my life and in my work, I already had all the attention I needed, and I was happy in those situations to be known just as "Catherine."

During the fifteen years I was a member of the Los Angeles Club before it closed, I often felt a quiet pleasure in knowing that many people I met there had doubtless read my books or been touched by my work in some way. I enjoyed knowing that many of them had also probably read my writings in *Science of Mind* Magazine.[19]

When I attended the closing luncheon of the club in 1991, thirty years after it was founded, the father of actor Tom Selleck was among those who spoke about their memories of the club's opening. One of his anecdotes was particularly memorable. He recalled that everyone excitedly anticipated a congratulatory telephone call from J. Paul Getty himself, who was in England at the time of the opening. The wealthy oilman made his call right on schedule, and *when* he made it, the elder Selleck remembered, he also lived up to his reputation—by calling collect!

WHO WOULD HAVE BELIEVED IT?

In the midst of all this socializing, my husband and I found ourselves listed in the Palm Springs-Palm Desert *Social Register*. We were described—along with such luminaries as former Ambassador and Mrs. Walter

---

19. *Science of Mind* Magazine, 3251 West Sixth St., Los Angeles, CA 90020-5096.

Annenberg, the Bob Hopes, former President and Mrs. Gerald Ford, and Mr. and Mrs. Leonard Firestone—as being among "the distinguished citizens of the desert." Also, soon after we arrived in Palm Springs to live, my *Who's Who*[20] listings began, and they have continued ever since.

In 1976, after twenty years' service to the Unity Movement, which included founding three churches, writing numerous books, and lecturing nationwide, a Doctorate was bestowed on me in special convention ceremonies. My long-time friend Dr. Ernest Wilson, known as "the dean of Unity ministers" and much revered by many, did the honors.

My son's grandmother, who had felt this country girl would never amount to anything, would scarcely have believed it was all possible. Nor would my husband's deceased father, who tended to feel much the same way about Bill. Will wonders ever cease?

MOTHER

I had always hoped the day would come when I could repay my mother for having helped me take care of my son when he was a child. I privately vowed that if the way ever opened, I would show my appreciation in an appropriate fashion.

That time arrived soon after Dr. Bill and I moved to Palm Springs. My father had passed on years earlier, and my brother and sister and their spouses had jobs that took them out of the country much of the time. So Mother was now living virtually alone.

---

20. *Who's Who in California, Who's Who in the West, Who's Who of American Women, Who's Who in Religion, Who's Who in Medicine and Healthcare, Who's Who in America,* and *Who's Who in the World.*

My husband and I decided to invite her to spend Christmases with us in Palm Springs. During her first such visit, she was intrigued with the area, appreciating the mild climate and loving the always-growing flowers of every variety. So I consulted with him about the possibility of our finding a nice little house for her, so she could come and live in the desert near part of her family—Dr. Bill and me. He immediately began looking for just the right house. Meanwhile, we said nothing to her about this, as she continued to fly in and spend each Christmas holiday with us.

After looking for two years, my husband said excitedly, "I think I've found the house." He had followed up on a small ad in the newspaper that was placed by the owner, who wanted to sell her house because she was leaving the area.

It was part of the Palm Desert Country Club community, had fruit trees in a fenced-in back yard, a nice back patio Mother could enjoy, and room for her beloved flower gardens. It seemed perfect!

On her birthday I called her and said, "Mother, I have a special birthday gift for you. If you would like to pull up stakes and come to Palm Springs to live, Bill and I feel we've found just the right house." Then I described it.

Without hesitation, she enthusiastically said "yes," and we set up a target date for moving her from the East Coast to the West Coast—in just six weeks!

After years of lonely widowhood, she would finally be able to have a stimulating, happy life again. How satisfying it was for me now to be able to show my appreciation for her past deeds and devotion, and in such a tangible way.

MY BEAUTIFICATION PROGRAM

She arrived by plane with little more than her luggage, having disposed of her household goods and furnishings before leaving. We celebrated her move by shopping for a new car and for new, desert-style furniture. Gradually I was able to get her out of the dark clothes she brought with her that gave her a perpetual "going to a funeral" look, replacing them with bright, colorful pants suits and several long dresses for evening wear at our various social events.

I had always wanted to "fix up" my mother. A tiny little lady who never weighed as much as a hundred pounds dripping wet, she looked adorable in those bright new pink, yellow, and even red clothes.

I found a beauty shop near her house where she could get her hair styled and where she got the first facial of her life, which took away years of dirt implanted in her skin as a result of gardening. And for the first time ever, I got her to wear makeup. She was delighted to see how her face looked with the subtle new shadings and accents.

She had always loved Yardley cosmetics—but not exactly for the reason most people did. Her appreciation of those cosmetics started with my first Christmas gift to her after I became a Government Girl in wartime Washington. I gave her an array of Yardley products, which represented an approach to personal grooming that she, given her simple lifestyle, had never thought much about. However, instead of using them, she placed them unopened on a shelf over the kitchen stove, along with the salt and pepper. Thereafter, everything she cooked smelled like those fragrant Yardley products!

I was determined that her desert cosmetics would come to no such end. So I personally helped apply her makeup whenever we went out for lunch, dinner, or a party. And—given all that care and color—the older she got, the cuter she became! She was at her most attractive in her early eighties when, compared to many seniors who tend to get overweight, she was a slender little doll.

Although "old age ain't no place for sissies," one can still blossom there, too. She did—at last. As one charm teacher has said, "The old, the young, and all the in-betweens can be perfectly adorable." She was.

How long I'd waited to see her blossom, and how gratified I was when it finally happened. By the time she passed on—in her sleep at the tender age of 85— she had rings on every finger, something she would never have considered until she got to the desert.

CELEBRATION TIME

Another thing she would never have considered before was what happened on her eightieth birthday.

I purposely made a fuss over all of her birthdays, since I couldn't remember anyone's ever having done so for her in my childhood. Now, living near us in the desert, she celebrated birthdays at the Old Pueblo Club in Tucson, the Racquet Club in Palm Springs, and other illustrious places around the West, where I was delighted to take her.

But perhaps her most memorable birthday celebration was her eightieth, which took place at the Arizona Biltmore Hotel in Phoenix. After we dined in their (then-named) Gold Room, my husband and I took her into the domed, Frank Lloyd Wright-designed "lounge." Some might have called it a "nightclub," but given her strict religious background, I didn't dare. Regardless of what we called it, this was a new experience for her.

A popular ragtime piano player named Big Tiny Little, who earlier in his career had worked with the Lawrence Welk Band, was onstage. When he asked for musical requests from the audience, my mother—whose first name was Kathleen—told us she wanted to hear the old Irish ballad my father had called his "courting song," which was, fittingly, "I'll Take You Home Again, Kathleen."

When we requested that Big Tiny Little play it for Mother, he replied coolly, without batting an eye, "Of course."

Then, not missing a beat, he and his musicians took off on a loud rock-and-roll tune I'd never heard before. Dr. Bill and I, not wanting Mother to be disappointed, thanked him enthusiastically when he finished, just as though he'd actually played the tune he obviously did not know.

Mother said, "That was a very strange rendition of 'my' song."

I casually replied, "You are right, Mother. I've never heard that version before, either. It must be the latest contemporary arrangement."

So my mother ushered in her eightieth birthday via rock-and-roll music in a lounge—or was it a nightclub? Her surroundings had been designed by Frank Lloyd Wright, but she was totally unimpressed. And though she was a good example of that affirmative statement people sometimes use to "jazz up" their lives—*The rest of my life is the best of my life*—I'm not sure she realized it . . . even that night!

MY ESTATE WORKPLACE

In 1980 I was feeling restless again. I had completed the first four books in my "Millionaires of the Bible" series, and I felt my world expanding to meet the expanded thinking those Biblical millionaires had imposed on me. I felt I had to have a larger place to live, one that would support the ever-greater and still-growing amount of work I was producing.

So Dr. Bill and I began our own private search in the historic old Las Palmas neighborhood, where decades before the Countess had told us we should live. In our search, we found a charming, Spanish-style hacienda that had gone into foreclosure and was available at a price we could manage. Within a short time, we'd closed the deal. Our new home consisted of a large main house and a guest house, which meant we had a place to live and I had a place to work. All the Spanish Colonial furniture we'd had custom-built in Mexico two decades earlier seemed to have been made for this hacienda.

After some remodeling and updating of the interior, we had sprinkler systems installed, landscaped the yard, and got outside walls built. This offered privacy and the added atmosphere of an estate. It was a living-in and working-in arrangement I was to enjoy for more than twenty years.

Only after we moved in did the neighbors tell us that our "estate" had been one of the Palm Springs properties of silent-screen comic Harold Lloyd, who starred in the era of Charlie Chaplin, Douglas Fairbanks, Sr., and Mary Pickford. (A television special once described him as "the Third Genius" in that group.) Years later, when I saw a write-up about and pictures of Harold Lloyd's Beverly Hills estate, I realized that it also was done in early Spanish Colonial style.

In the area were the estates of Kirk Douglas, Gene Autry, Mario Lanza, and Dinah Shore, as well as that of Warner Brothers Studio. The house next door to us was a second home to the Lew Wassermans. He was known both on Wall Street and in Hollywood as "Mr. Show

Business" and in that era was regarded as the most powerful person in his profession.

Although most residents of the Palm Springs area think nothing of profuse name-dropping (or "name dripping," as one person called it), no one had mentioned these illustrious past or present neighbors when we bought what finally became "Catherine's Casa."

THE PROPAGANDA THAT BACKFIRED

In an article on Palm Springs, I was amazed to read the author's claim that "even the maids in Palm Springs drive Cadillacs."

"Nonsense," I thought. "Somebody has really gotten carried away with their Palm Springs hype."

Then one day, as I went out the front gate of our walled property and walked over to where I'd parked my car prior to a planned outing, I was amazed to see an old but very respectable-looking Cadillac parked there, too. I thought, "What's that car doing in front of my wall?" We needed the area for my own staff's vehicle parking.

I assumed it must belong to one of my neighbors, even though they all had space in front of their own walls for such purposes. I was indignant—until it hit me. A very quiet, efficient maid was working for me that day. Upon inquiry I found out *that* car belonged to her.

Not only did I discover that Palm Springs maids *do*, on occasion, drive Cadillacs, but I also found out that my *own* maid drove one! So much for my evaluation of "Palm Springs propaganda."

A TRAUMATIC CHANGE

After my husband and I had been happily married for over fifteen years, he began to feel bad both physically and emotionally, and also to behave differently. He told me he didn't know what was going on, but said he just didn't feel right.

He'd suffered from various ailments since childhood, which later, in his search for well-being and effective treatment, led him to chiropractic—and relief. On this occasion, however, I suggested he get a complete physical from our long-time medical doctor. He agreed.

When he returned from the doctor's office, he said, "Apparently it's my medication. It needs changing."

But despite the change he made, his uncharacteristic behavior continued. He just wasn't the Dr. Bill I had always known and enjoyed. When his sense of humor gradually started to diminish, I knew he *really* did not feel well. But he insisted it was a phase that would pass.

It did not.

Then, curiously, I began to have dreams in which he was gone. I also began feeling as though whatever lessons we had come together to learn and share with each other were over—complete. These feelings were not what I wanted; they simply "appeared." I could not explain or understand where they came from. But years of working with people's challenges and struggles had taught me that life's mysteries frequently are not easily understood—especially from a short-term perspective.

I did not want our marriage to be over. I had believed from childhood that ideally a person marries once—for life—and when a problem appears, you search for what's wrong and work to fix it. However, as he continued to undergo change, I realized I had no choice but to release him mentally and acknowledge that I could not compel him to have the thoughts and feelings I wanted him to have. I knew he could only do as he saw fit, and my "release" was an acknowledgment that I could not stand in his way, even if I wanted to.

I was not shocked when he gradually began talking divorce.

I said, "For me, divorce is not an option. Medical help is. Let's find out what's wrong and get it fixed."

By then, ours was a marriage of almost twenty years' duration. Nevertheless, I affirmed to myself and to him that he should do what he felt was best, though I told him I would never initiate a divorce.

Our lawyer, who had been a good friend to both of us, was disturbed by Dr. Bill's attitude as well as by his untreated health problems. Bill, in his restlessness, left the area. Ultimately he initiated a dissolution process, since I would not. His surface complaint was: "She never found the kitchen." My response? "Guilty as charged." (But I *do* make one great thing: dinner reservations.)

Some time later, his married daughter telephoned me from out of state to say that Bill had passed on as a consequence of multiple health problems. In comforting her, I found comfort for myself as well. Later, when Bill appeared to me in dreams, I saw him looking well and happy again, which helped me immensely to attain the final release I needed. I was further comforted by and saw the great wisdom in that old saying, "A death can be a healing."

Had life thrown me another curve? Maybe so, but there was nothing to do other than to "pick myself up, dust myself off, and start all over again."

Only after he was gone did I realize what a strain the previous years had been. I'd had "too many balls in the air." I'd tried to do a balancing act with my global work, my writing, caring for my mother, supervising the staff at home and in the office, and struggling to deal with my husband's health problems and increasingly unpredictable personality.

Even so, as in past marriages that ended, I could never completely let down physically or emotionally, for too much depended upon my living and working as normally as possible. Although that requirement was an added strain, it proved to be a blessing, because it kept drawing me back to the higher way of thinking and acting I had been writing about for so many years. More than ever, I needed these inspirational teachings in order to go on.

My desert staff and my East Coast family tried in their own way to support me emotionally. It was not the easiest of times for any of us, but it was necessary. "My growing was showing."

I was especially comforted by these old sayings: "All that is done against me helps me" and "Those who are with us in understanding can't leave us. Those who are not with us can't stay!"

A GODSEND

During this period, someone came back into my life whom I had not seen in many years. My goddaughter Jenny. When I first met her years earlier, I felt she was the daughter I never had. So she became my "spiritual daughter," just as the charming, now-deceased, senior Mrs. Ponder had become my "spiritual mother."

Later, Jenny went to Washington, D.C., to work, and she also studied at night to earn a graduate degree. Years after that, with her second degree in hand, she landed in Southern California. She was even more charming than before—and a very well-educated young lady who was now one of the few women executives in her industry. She began spending occasional weekends and some holidays with me, resuming the happy relationship we enjoyed decades before. She remembered Dr. Bill and had experienced his maverick personality, so we talked of many things I could not comfortably discuss with anyone else. (Dr. Bill's early reaction to Jenny had been, "Catherine, we've got to be careful of that goddaughter of yours, or she may 'sweet-sweet' us to death." I'm happy that Jenny is still in the "sweet-sweet" business. It has carried her far.)

Five years after coming to Southern California, Jenny was offered an excellent job back in Washington, D.C. She spent a weekend telling me about it, saying, "I'm extremely reluctant to leave you out here by yourself."

I said, "Think nothing of it. You appeared when I needed you most. *God knows and God shows.*"

But Jenny was right. I *was* "out there by myself," for by that time, my little mother had quietly passed on. During the last year of her life we spent much pleasant time together. Just as I once worked to bring her out of herself, she had begun wanting to produce a similar result in me, saying she believed it was time for me "to come out and play" the way she imagined I might want to.

Jenny has continued to be a part of my extended family. As opportunities have presented themselves, we've spent various vacations and holidays together in California, Washington, D.C., and places in between.

Various long-term friends and members of my staff have also been a Godsend to me through the ups and downs of my life, by also acting as members of my extended family.

HOW TO GET THROUGH TRANSITIONAL TIMES

One of the first inspirational phrases I ever heard was "Welcome change and call it good." That simple statement has carried me through many an unforeseen experience. And as I was moving through those experiences, I often drew encouragement from another well-known statement, which I've usually heard from psychologists: "Life may be hard by the yard, but by the inch, it's a cinch."

CHAPTER 12

The Lecture Outreach Saga

Although I never cared for the lecture platform, preferring to do research and writing, I had no choice. Lecturing went with the territory I had entered. It required a terrific discipline that I apparently needed for my own growth, and it contributed significantly to my understanding of the people who were interested in subjects I covered in my books.

AN ART FORM DEVELOPS

Giving public talks, of course, is part of what every minister expects to do, and training for it is part of every minister's education. When I attended public-speaking classes in Ministerial School in the 1950s, the instructor was from the University of Kansas. Though satisfied with my overall ability as a speaker, she had been concerned about my distinct Southern accent. She thought something was wrong with my speaking the way I did, and she tried to "fix it." I even tried to help her though I silently thought, "Just what part of 'Y'all' don't you understand?" But the harder we tried to fix my accent, the worse it got.

Finally she gave up, saying compassionately, "Unity School will never send you anywhere to speak except the South, because nobody else could understand you."

Because I accepted her verdict as true, I came into the ministry, and later into nationwide lecture work, with troubling reservations about my ability to speak, feeling my Southern accent was a liability.

Instead, it proved to be among my greatest assets. People didn't always remember *what* I said, but they remembered *how* I said it. Someone has observed, "Talking Southern is an art form." Had that speech teacher foreseen that I was destined to receive invitations to speak to audiences from every level of society around the world, she would have been astounded.

Some years later, I received a long distance call in my San Antonio offices from a lady in Seattle, Washington. A few weeks later, I lectured there and appeared on a noontime television news show. That same lady turned on the program just in time to hear me being interviewed. She said excitedly to a friend nearby, "That's Catherine Ponder."

"How do you know? You've never seen her," said the friend.

"True. But I've talked to her on the telephone and I'd know that voice and that accent anywhere."

Often when I've lectured, people have asked, "Why don't your books have a Southern accent?"

My answer? "They do, but my 'Yankee editor' just keeps cutting it out."

THE HEIGHTS AND THE DEPTHS

When I began to write about prosperity, I never anticipated the heights and depths to which it would take me. I've followed dog acts on television (not once, but several times). I've had to kiss babies and allow myself to be kissed on the cheek by persons who were not babies. Someone once quipped, "That's hard work, but somebody's gotta do it."

I stayed in run-down motels and rode in the coach or economy sections of buses and airplanes—until my now-adult son saw what I was going through. He got me into better hotels and saw that I flew first-class. He knew what a difference that would make, since I often took a flight on Sunday afternoon, just after completing my own services. Then I flew through various time zones and changes of climate and weather—only to be expected to be ready early the next morning for day-long interviews and other commitments, at all of which I was supposed to be fresh, looking good, and sparkling. Further, the seminar work itself meant standing on my feet two hours a night for several consecutive nights, then autographing books and answering endless questions, all the time smiling and being affable.

Although I lectured in many beautiful cities, I usually saw only the airport, my hotel room, and the lecture hall. More often than not, I worked with total strangers in whatever conditions they provided, and had to adjust accordingly and harmoniously. I sometimes enjoyed an interchange of ideas and experiences with my hosts; at other times there was none.

As soon as I returned from those lecture trips, I was expected to hit the ground running and once more meet the demands of my own ministry, without ever missing a beat. Never mind jet lag. Never mind a weary body or a tired mind.

That lifestyle may have appeared to be very glamorous to onlookers, but it included some of the hardest work I ever did—physically, mentally, and emotionally.

Despite its strains, the work of teaching and writing about prosperity opened bright new vistas to me that would never have been available had I remained only in the pastoral ministry—even though I loved that phase of my work. Having a "specialty" that addressed the profound needs of people everywhere made me feel, as an author, as though the whole world was welcoming me with opened arms, because everyone desires prosperity in some form—as actual monetary wealth or more generally as increased peace, health, and love—as "wholeness."

A more serious difficulty developed when, to my considerable surprise, I was severely criticized during the early years by those who said, "Oh, she's just after money."

How did I handle that? I said nothing, and I simply declared for my critics, *Jesus Christ now heals all critical states of mind.* The criticism gradually died down and was replaced with appreciation and respect. Those critics have long since been "outta here."

Another serious difficulty in my work has been what some psychologists term "the dark side of success." I wish someone had warned me about it, though I found out about it soon enough from experience. In plain English, it involves the spontaneous appearance of gold diggers, who show up either in a business guise, as personal friends, or even (as some do!) in the name of love. In the latter case, what remains is for one to discover that, yes, they are in love—not with you, but with your financial assets. My son and I were both required to confront and deal with the gold-digger syndrome.

FROM THE BEGINNING

In 1956, I started my lecture work with classes, following them in 1957 with local weekend and midweek talks. By 1960, I had begun doing lecture work at both professional and business conventions and, once I got to Texas, I was doing dozens of lectures all over the Southwest. By the mid-1960s, I had begun lecturing in most of major cities of the United States.

Often these were convention talks for the International New Thought Alliance (INTA),[21] an organization noted for presenting many of the best-known inspirational speakers and writers. Frequently, after speaking for the INTA, I gave parties to thank my coworkers and the other speakers for promoting my books. Among the many notable places I gave such parties were the Waldorf-Astoria Hotel, New York; the El Coronado Hotel, San Diego; the Fontainebleau Hotel, Miami Beach; the Royal Hawaiian Hotel (also known as the "Pink Palace"), Honolulu; the Phoenix (Arizona) Country Club; and the Brown-Palace Hotel, Denver. I discovered that, for public relations purposes, those parties were just as important as my lectures. Of course, they were all done quite aside from the usual work I did and the talks I gave to my own ministry and to other Unity groups, as well as to churches in the Religious Science and Divine Science movements and various secular groups.

From coast to coast, I also gave radio, television, and print-media interviews. Nor did I always remain in this country: at a Canadian Chiropractic Convention, I lectured with a member of Parliament. At a Unity World Conference in England, I was not only the Keynote Speaker but I also gave an international party for attendees and their translators, who had come from all over the world. The eminent Sir John Templeton was the Guest of Honor.

---

21. The International New Thought Alliance headquarters, 5003 E. Broadway Rd., Mesa, AZ, 85206, USA.

MEMORABLE LECTURE EXPERIENCES

NEW YORK: Among my most memorable experiences was lecturing at Town Hall, New York, for Dr. Raymond Charles Barker. Sitting down front was my literary agent, along with my New York editor. When I introduced my editor, he arose, went out into the middle aisle, turned around, waved at the audience, and blew them kisses. I had a hard time getting him settled down and seated again so we could proceed with the lecture. Afterward, he continued to take bows at the autographing table. He was having such a good time that I asked him to help autograph my books. I didn't have the heart to "rain on his parade." Never mind my own . . . .

RENO: Another unforgettable experience was lecturing at the gold-domed Pioneer Theater Auditorium in Reno, Nevada. A local businessman who had given my book *The Dynamic Laws of Prosperity* to many hundreds of his business associates insisted that I speak there, so he—and they—could meet me in person. I was amazed to see him crowd in more than a thousand of his "best friends" for the lecture in those elegant, gold-dust surroundings.

Afterward, he insisted on walking me through the various casinos, so that many of my readers who had to work at the gambling tables and could not get away to attend my lecture could wave at me while continuing to do their jobs. Gambling has never been one of my interests, but *those* casinos I couldn't help but love.

CHICAGO: In the 1960s and early 1970s, I conducted a number of prosperity lectures for the popular Dr. Johnnie Colemon at her Christ Universal Temple, then located on South State Street. She and I first studied together at Unity School in the 1950s, had been ordained together, and afterward were to become life-time friends.

On one trip, in the morning before my lecture that night, she said, "Ponder, let's go down to Marshall Field's store and look around."

Upon our arrival, I was somehow drawn toward the diamond counter.

When Johnnie realized where I was headed, she said in a firm voice, "Ponder, stay away from there."

Startled, I slunk away, while the clerks, the security officer, the customers, and heaven knows who else looked at me as though I were a diamond thief, and Johnnie was saving the day for them.

After we left the store, I asked, "Johnnie, why did you do that to me?"

"Ponder," she said, "I have a problem with you and diamonds."

I was puzzled. "How can that be? I don't even *have* any diamonds?"

She said, "The problem is that every time you come to town and lecture on prosperity, members of my congregation give me diamonds—mostly diamond rings. And each one expects me to wear *their* diamond. I have a drawer full of diamond rings. The last thing I need is for you to look at the diamonds in the Marshall Field's display and visualize them. You'll just open the way for more diamonds to come to me. I've got too many now."

I said a silent prayer. "*God, don't get me wrong. I'm delighted that Johnnie's congregation is so generous and that she's got all those diamond rings. But what about me? I'm the one who wrote the books.*"

After the lecture that night, as I was finishing up at the autographing table, here came Johnnie. Once more, she seemed exasperated with me.

"Ponder, you did it again. Only tonight I was given not one, but *two* diamond rings."

I thought, *"Some problem."*

In middle-age, when my diamonds did arrive, the first one came from one of the world's premiere stores, known for its diamonds: Tiffany's of Beverly Hills, California—thanks to Dr. Bill. But back in those days with Johnnie, I just reminded myself: "The longer your good is in coming, the bigger it will be when it comes, so hang on."

I also have a confession to make. Even though that "diamond event" with Johnnie happened more than thirty years ago, I've never had the courage to put my foot in Marshall Field's Chicago store since! I think you know why.

TEXAS PIONEERS

I went to the "United States of Texas" for two weeks and stayed twelve years. Did all the blood, sweat, and tears of pioneering two new churches in Central Texas prove fruitful in the long term? Absolutely. I often joked with Reverend Jean Amos, who pioneered the first Religious Science Church in Dallas—and for whom I lectured from time to time—that Sam Houston and Stephen F. Austin had nothing on us, since we were Texas pioneers, too!

In that part of the country these days, there are many ministers of Unity, Religious Science, and Divine Science as well as some independents who came out of either my Austin or San Antonio ministries; or in some cases the *students* of my students became ministers. The result is that Texas has numerous churches or study groups that were founded after I left the area, many of which nevertheless tie in with my early lecture work there.

I wore out two cars driving around the great Southwest, speaking for other groups. One friend who remembers me from that era has said, "The first time I ever met you, you were driving a tired Chevrolet." I didn't go on to confess that more than my car was tired. But now, in retrospect, I can see that all of my efforts were worth it.

A TRUE "TEXAS TALL TALE"

The way Reverend Jean Amos used the power of thought to achieve results was a great lesson to me. When she felt guided to leave California and go to Dallas to found its Religious Science church, she had no money and knew no one in "Big D." So she got a day job there while concentrating nightly on the basic Religious Science textbook, *The Science of Mind,* by Dr. Ernest Holmes.[22] For an entire year, during every spare minute, she immersed herself in the positive, uplifting truths she found in that book and in the use of "spiritual mind treatment"—affirmative prayer—for the church she envisioned.

After that year, she had progressed enough to start a Science of Mind study group, which quickly grew into her first congregation of fifty people. They met in a small chapel and she used a tiny adjoining office for counseling and for displaying books and literature. I lectured for her group in that chapel, just off of the North Central Expressway.

At the time, she said to me with great confidence, "Dallas is growing north. I expect to have a nice church filled with Dallas millionaires, and I am doing spiritual

---

22. *The Science of Mind,* by Ernest Holmes (1938; 1998, Tarcher/Putnam, New York).

mind treatment every day for that." Within five years, I lectured in the church her growing congregation had just bought in North Dallas. One of her millionaire Board members and his wife entertained me in their home afterward.

When I invited Jean to speak to my Austin group and tell them how she had managed such a feat, she arrived in a private plane piloted by one of her Board members. That same night, after her lecture, she and her millionaire pilot and his wife returned to Dallas in his plane.

She remained Dallas-deep in millionaires until her retirement back to the West Coast some years later.

A TALLER TEXAS TALE

A former student of mine talked her way into Ministerial School at the tender age of sixty, shortly after her husband's death. Since officials at the school were not sure they could place her after she finished her training, she took matters into her own hands.

She offered to speak for a Unity group in West Texas that was meeting in rented quarters, but also praying regularly for their own church building. However, the general assumption of both the congregation and the Board of Trustees, given their West Texas outlook, was that they wouldn't even consider selecting a woman as their minister.

Nevertheless, after speaking before the congregation, who liked her, she met with the Board of Trustees. She got their attention immediately when she said, "If I were to take this church, I want you to know that from August through January, I'd have to give a short talk and conclude the entire service promptly by noon on Sundays, because I am an avid football fan, and I promise you we'd all be home in time for the kickoff of whatever game you wanted to watch!" Then she added in a hushed, hesitant manner, "Also, I must confess to you that I have nothing against a person having a bit of bourbon and branch water on occasion."

Obviously she knew her West Texans, for those trustees conferred for no more than twenty seconds before enthusiastically announcing that she had been hired—unanimously.

When she built a church and got it paid off in just four short years, I asked her how she had managed to produce such an amazing result.

She proudly replied, "I have the only church in our movement built by goats."

"Goats?"

"Yes. People think Texas wealth is all tied up in cattle and oil. But Angora goats can make you rich, too. I have some members who shared their 'mohair money,' and a paid-for church is the result."

That reminded me of an affirmation I have often used: *God provides His own amazing channels of supply to me now.*

But through *goats?*

Does God have a sense of humor, or what?

A TEXAN'S VERSION OF THE BIBLE

Once when I was lecturing on the "Millionaires of Genesis," I mentioned that Abraham was a millionaire. A startled Texas businessman cautiously asked, "*If* Abraham was a millionaire, how many oil wells did he have?"

With a prayer in my heart I replied, "I don't know, but I'll find out." When I checked the description of Abraham's wealth in the book of Genesis, I could not locate a single oil well for him.

I thought, "This will never do." So I carefully re-studied the passages describing his wealth. I was relieved to find one verse that stood out like a neon light: "Abraham was very rich in *cattle*, in silver and in gold." (Genesis 13:2)

When I reported to the skeptical Texan that Abraham had been a rich *cattleman*, he was so impressed that he decided Abraham was not only a millionaire but a "Texas millionaire"—and that Abraham's cattle had probably been "Longhorn steers"—as found in the Lone Star State! Since this man's slogan was "Don't mess with Texas," I did not dare comment on his "revised Texas version of the Bible."

SHE MADE OUR DAY!

Among the hundreds of Texas lectures I gave over the years, one that caused some of the most excitement was not memorable because of anything I said. It was memorable because, as I was speaking from my book *The Dynamic Laws of Prosperity*, Miss Ima Hogg arrived in her chauffeured limousine.

The Hogg name, which I'd heard since the day I arrived in Texas, was magic in the state. Her father, James Hogg, had been a colorful Governor of Texas, whose family amassed a fortune in oil. And "Miss Ima" (as she was generally called) was not only the bearer of that celebrated family name but she was also a well-known philanthropist. She eventually donated the home owned by her and her brother, which was filled with art of the American West, to the Houston Museum of Fine Art.

Several of the people who were assisting me that morning began speculating quietly that perhaps Miss Ima intended to leave us a gift. "Otherwise," I heard among their whispers, "why would one of the best-

known, wealthiest women in Texas show up at a prosperity lecture?" (Another "possibility" I overheard from
a man who loved frontier art was that maybe she would
give us a piece from her famous Frederic Remington
collection.)

By that time in my life, however, I understood that
prosperity comes in many forms, and that the gift of
someone's *presence* rather than their *presents* may be the
real abundance they have to offer. So other than finding those rumors mildly amusing as they circulated
among the staff, I gave them no attention. Indeed, Miss
Ima's lasting gift to me and to my Houston audience
that morning did turn out simply to be that she was
there—giving us all a wonderful memory of a well-
known Texas lady who'd made our day.

A LOVE STORY CONTINUES

As for the church Kelly Ponder and I founded in
1961, I returned to it in 1991 for a Thirtieth
Anniversary celebration. The minister there graciously
arranged for a festive banquet and my Sunday morning
talk to be held in a local hotel ballroom.

People came from near and far for the weekend.
Austin had grown so much that I could no longer see
the University tower or the dome of the State Capitol
from my rooms high atop our hotel. Too many tall
buildings had been erected in between. But any small
disappointments about the changed skyline were more
than balanced out by the estimated one thousand people who later crowded into the ballroom. The audience
loved learning that the founding of Unity of Austin had
been based on a love story.

All that Kelly Ponder, his study group, and our later
Unity of Austin congregation prayed for and pictured

had come true. Today there is not just one, but there are several Unity groups in the Capital City. Religious Science is represented there as well. And other similar groups meet nearby. Indeed, Kelly's and my love story—in the form of inspirational thinking—continues today to grow in the heart of Texas.

AN UNFORGETTABLE 40TH ANNIVERSARY

In 1996, after having lived and worked in the desert for a number of years, I conducted a series of "40th Anniversary Lectures." In presenting these, I returned to the groups that helped launch me as a minister and writer in the 1950s, when they had no idea what my potential was—and neither did I.

This meant I returned to Palm Beach; New Orleans; Chicago; Houston; Sacramento; Founder's Church of Religious Science in Los Angeles; Unity School, in Unity Village, Missouri; and various conferences and conventions. All were memorable experiences in which I was able to honor many ministers—whether they were active, retired, or had passed on—who had supported and encouraged me early in my own ministry.

Among these gratifying experiences, perhaps the most spectacular was when I returned to the site of my first ministry—Unity Church of Birmingham, Alabama—where the minister, his wife, and staff had arranged an elegant "gold-dust banquet" in my honor.

I had originally arrived in Birmingham in 1956 with my young son and $30. Now, in 1996, I returned with my grown-up son along with an international reputation as an author and founder of several ministries that have reached worldwide. Two attendees of my original 1958 prosperity class and members of their families also attended as my special guests. They had flown in from Indiana and New York.

Had their attendance at my first prosperity class paid off? One had earned a Doctorate in Journalism and was now a Professor Emeritus. The other had married into a wealthy East Coast family and now, as a widow, lived on the family estate.

Unity School acknowledged the Birmingham celebration by sending, as their representative, the head of Unity's International Department. He had traveled the world setting up new groups and serving those already established. During his remarks at the banquet, he noted that in doing his work, he had been thrilled to find my books scattered worldwide. He added that many people who attend Unity groups internationally had told him that their introduction to inspirational thinking had been through my books. The Unity School representative honored me with Unity's "Good Will Ambassador to the World" Award.

Then the President of the Association of Unity Churches, Dr. Glenn Mosley, presented me with a 40-Year Service Award. It was especially meaningful coming from Dr. Mosley, since I had known him for lo those forty years.

And finally, the Mayor's office presented me with keys to the city. Because Kelly Ponder had been born in Birmingham, those symbolic keys took on a special meaning for me.

The next morning at the Sunday service, the two original prosperity class members from 1956 and I were able to rejoice further in the growth of that church. It was now no longer in the old Southern mansion I liked so much, as it had moved into a new building on the same property. But the loving, standing-room-only audience that morning was all we had pictured it being—forty years before.

Both the minister and I felt the strong presence of an unseen force of people that dated back to the church's beginnings in the 1920s. They were, we felt, in a rejoicing mood as they looked on from the next plane of life. It was as though the church was crowded with an enthusiastic, packed-house audience we could see, and then one just as full, consisting of early members who were also there, that we could not see. We jointly felt they almost crowded us off the platform.

It was "icing on the cake" when the musicians ended that celebratory meeting by playing "Stars Fell on Alabama," the song that brought me to that church in the first place!

MEMORABLE MOMENTS

Meeting and working with Dr. Marcus Bach, retired Professor of Religion from Iowa State University, and author of several dozen books on the world's various religions was a delight, as we conducted a seminar together.

Meeting and hearing the famed Adelle Davis, popular nutritionist and writer, tell a group of "movers and shakers" at a convention that they needed to take as good care of their bodies, as of their minds, sent me home to include vitamins and herbs in my diet.

IN SUMMARY, WHAT A TRIP!

In the final analysis, my "gold-dust prosperity seminars" had taken me from their beginnings on the Gold Coast of Florida for Unity to the glamour of Beverly Hills for Science of Mind—with various secular convention/college/business/professional groups in between. My lecture saga over those forty years – what an education, what a bonus, what a trip it all had been!

CHAPTER 13

A Fifty-Year Writing Saga—Part I
From the East Coast through Texas

Once when I lectured in New Orleans, the title of my talk, taken from my book *The Prosperity Secrets of the Ages*, was "You Can Have Everything." After the lecture started, a businessman came rushing in from work. As he dashed past the usher, he said breathlessly, "I hope I'm not too late, because I'm here to 'get everything.'"

Many people may be attracted to a book or even hurry to a lecture after work if they think it can show them how to get everything. One person declared, "What she writes is not so different. What *is* different is the way she makes it all hang together." Someone else put it more directly: "Catherine Ponder has an obsession about the subject of prosperity."

All of which brings up another question I have been asked constantly over the years: how did I come to be a writer at all—and why have I focused so consistently on the subject of prosperity?

THE BEGINNING

I considered it one of life's small victories that day in the 1950s when I rushed home to show my parents the check I'd just received from Unity School, confirming its having accepted my first article for publication. The check was for $12, but it felt like a million to me. The look of astonishment on my father's face, and my mother's unbelief, were priceless.

What they did not know until then was that for the previous two years, an inspirational idea had been welling up in my mind and would not go away. Finally I remembered to ask for Divine Guidance. My question was simple: "What am I supposed to do with this idea?"

The answer had astounded me: "Write it as an article and send it to the editor of the Unity publications for review."

I quietly slaved away over that article for a long time. When I finally felt it was as well-crafted as I knew how to make it, I submitted it to the editor, though I worried that the whole effort was rather foolish. I explained in the accompanying letter that I had no writing training or experience, and that I would understand perfectly if he refused the article—but that I'd had to follow my strong feelings by showing it to him.

He responded with a cordial letter of congratulations *and* that $12 check. I was on my way as a published author!

The next article took me six months to write and get accepted for publication. But after that, the process slowly got easier as I learned, painstakingly and intuitively, how to express myself on paper. I was still a legal secretary, with a boss who was meticulous about every word that went on paper. Neither of us realized it, but by his being that way, he was helping me develop my literary abilities. And writing out the Correspondence Course lessons for Unity Training School took me a step closer to recognizing what I truly cared about, since I found that inspirational writing interested me most. No wonder they said at that first retreat I attended, "You are here by Divine Appointment." But even they could not have known how far that Divine

Appointment was later to take my work through the written word—and that it would ultimately spread worldwide.

As I did more and more writing, my "workplaces" slowly reflected my improvement and success. I wrote my first articles at the end of my mother's kitchen table, which was covered with an oil-cloth tablecloth. Then I progressed to the end of her dining room table, with its linen tablecloth. Finally I made it to my own small portable electric typewriter, with which I often wrote in the middle of the night, in my bedroom.

THE NEXT STEP

After I went to Unity of Birmingham and had begun teaching my first prosperity class, I sat at the typewriter in my "gold-dust study" in that old Southern mansion one Sunday afternoon following the service, while my son played baseball outside. There, rather casually, I threw together a short article about the results that were experienced by those who attended my first prosperity class. The article was entitled "Your Success Is Unlimited."

In 1959, when it was published in *Good Business* magazine (a Unity publication that is no longer in print), the editor wrote me excitedly that he got more reader reaction to that article than to anything that had appeared in a long time. He urged me to keep writing on the subject. So, for the next five years, one of my prosperity articles appeared in almost every issue of that magazine. It made my name a household word in the Unity Movement, and invitations to lecture on prosperity began pouring in from everywhere.

WRITING METHODS FROM AUSTIN

After writing most of my first book, *The Dynamic Laws of Prosperity*, in my gold-dust study in Birmingham, I continued work on it in the apartment overlooking the University of Texas in Austin where Kelly Ponder and I lived. There I completed that book, and he edited it. This was followed by my writing *The Prosperity Secrets of the Ages.*

After his death, I was unable to write creatively for a year. Nothing came from within. Finally *The Dynamic Laws of Healing* emerged, in a hurry, from notes I had made previously, over a long period of time. It quickly and quietly became a bestseller, as people studied it—especially the first four chapters—and got results.

My method of writing was to shut myself up each summer in that apartment after my lecture season was over. There I wrote a chapter a week for twelve weeks, thus completing another book. Then I returned to my lecture schedule, locally and throughout the country, for the fall/winter/spring seasons. When I took my show on the road to do lecture work, I billed it as "Have Books, Will Travel."

In meeting people on the road, I heard all kinds of viewpoints. One skeptic said, "I've read some of your books, and nothing's happened yet. I don't think all those good things you write about really happen to people. I think you make them up."

I thought to myself, *"If I did, I wouldn't be in the self-help business. I'd be making millions as a novelist or show-business writer."*

When I asked that man how long he had been reading my books, he replied offhandedly, "Oh, about two weeks."

So I suggested he keep at it and give the ideas more time to work. I explained that he needed the *inworking* before he could have an *outworking.*

My writing method—and the reason I always had plenty of authentic stories to write about—was deceptively simple. I chose a subject that people seemed interested in and probably needed help with. Then I did research and gave some lectures or classes about it. As the attendees used the ideas and reported their good results, either in person or through letters, I gathered those results in a file with other such reports. When I had enough material, I was ready to start my summer's writing.

But that didn't mean the work was *easy.* My Austin maid, who used to see me writing when she came to clean the apartment, was among those who didn't realize how strenuous such work could be. On occasion, she observed to her friends, "Professor Ponder's wife does not write books. She spits them out through her typewriter."

THE BOOK I DID NOT WANT TO WRITE

The Healing Secrets of the Ages was the one book I did not want to write. I had research notes that I'd developed, first in Birmingham and later in Austin, but the subject seemed too hard for me to tackle. So I tried everything I knew to avoid writing it.

But the "twelve powers of the mind" I described in that book would not leave me alone until I took my research files and painstakingly explained each mind power, chapter by chapter, and related what it could do if a person were willing to apply it. The results have been satisfying both for me and my readers. Many people have brought powerful, positive change into their lives as a consequence of their fascination with the twelve powers of the mind I discussed in *The Healing Secrets of the Ages.*

One young lady appeared at an out-of-state lecture I was giving and said, "My mother had planned to be here for your prosperity seminar. She had been in very bad health, but her study of your two healing books brought about such good results that she is now on a trip to Europe celebrating! She sends you her best regards."

I learned that a young man and his wife were passing through some library stacks when one of my books seemed just to sail off of a shelf and hit him on the head. When he opened it, he discovered it contained exactly the ideas he needed right then.

People have often found the Ponder books in other unusual ways. One lady had a vivid dream. The only thing she remembered from it later was the name that kept appearing there: "Catherine Ponder." When she asked—first her family, then her coworkers—if anyone knew the name, she found that no one did. But someone suggested she check the library for published authors, just in case. There she found a list of my books and rushed to her bookstore to get one—which was just the *right* book for her at that point. It would seem that divine ideas have their own mysterious ways of reaching people when the time is appropriate.

THE BOOK I ALMOST LOST MY RELIGION OVER

Ironically, the book I almost lost my religion over was, of all things, my book on prayer, which was originally entitled *Pray and Grow Rich* by my publisher. I practically came to blows with my then New York editor over that sacred subject.

One would never have known I'd even heard of the word "prayer" by the time I finished losing my cool with him. That editor wanted to cut two chapters out of my precious book, probably because of length and for economic reasons. And indeed he did.

I never wrote for him again.

Instead, many years later when I had changed publishers, that newer publisher was kind enough to allow me to reinsert those two chapters. It made a larger but far more complete book on the subject, retitled *The Dynamic Laws of Prayer.*

A reader later wrote, "How fortunate you were to find a publisher who allowed you to include those two previously left-out chapters. They are some of the most important and enlightening in the book."

Some years later, when that New York editor and his wife retired to Florida, he wrote reminding me he had been my "Yankee editor"—as though I could forget him. (He was also, of course, the editor with whom I'd gone around and around over my Southern accent, which disturbed him when it kept creeping into my writing.)

In spite of our past differences, by the time he retired, either he had mellowed or I had. Regardless, we shed our differences and became friends again. Only this time, he complimented me for the "Southern charm" he claimed radiated from little notes I sometimes mailed to him. Was that his way of making things right from the past? I don't know and I don't care. But I did finally realize what a remarkable editor he had been to put up with me through the several books I wrote from Austin. I was glad for our joint peace at last.

THE BOOK I DID NOT WANT PUBLISHED

Another irony has been that the book I did not even want published—*The Prospering Power of Love*—became a perennial bestseller. My Unity editor wanted to take a series of my articles and put them together as a book. I finally agreed, reluctantly, that the articles I had written on love would be the best to develop for such a project.

But I was not happy with how it turned out, for I always felt it was somewhat disjointed and not like a book one plans chapter by chapter. Regardless, *The Prospering Power of Love* just seemed to "happen," since it is a subject most readers are interested in. Soon in this new millennium, I intend to expand it into a larger book.

Regardless of my private feelings, *The Prospering Power of Love,* according to reports that have come back to me, led to some great results, especially in the field of love, marriage, and relationships—when happy developments came about or emotional difficulties were resolved. In one class based on that book, so many people got married and left town that the class had to be dissolved!

Also, the "Writing to the Angel" prayer method I described in that book is certainly in tune with the present times, when so much interest exists in angels as messengers from On High. Writing to one's angel, or Higher Self, or that of someone who is having problems or is causing you problems, then watching the fruitful turn-around results, is always a delight. It works in all kinds of situations, such as politics, the weather, travel, health, and prosperity, as well as for love in its many forms.

The chairman of the Board of Trustees of a prominent church where I was receiving an award came over quietly at a luncheon in my honor and said, "I have a friend who was told that, because of a technicality, she could not collect any of the $60,000 that was owed to her on insurance claims for damage to her home. But she was undaunted, and she began to write daily to the Angel of each person involved. She got her $60,000!"

Regardless of what one uses this prayer method for, it brings a wondrous sense of peace. And a sense of peace indicates answered prayer—an answer that's here now . . . or one that's on the way.

The books I've just mentioned are primarily the ones I wrote from Austin, Texas, in the 1960s.

BOOKS WRITTEN FROM THE ALAMO CITY

Among the books I have authored, one of my favorites is *Open Your Mind to Prosperity,* which I wrote soon after arriving in the Alamo City of Texas: San Antonio. Perhaps the reason I like the book so much is that I had refined my prosperity material during ten years on the lecture circuit. That gave me a chance to fine-tune everything I had previously heard and learned, and to record the many results that people shared with me. The result? It is a simplified version of everything I've learned on the subject.

The companion to that one is *Open Your Mind to Receive,* a book I developed in my furnished apartment in San Antonio, though it did not get into print until after I went to Palm Springs. It has been equally as popular, probably because the introduction and chapter one especially show a reader how to receive.

A well-known self-help guru, often seen on television and the lecture circuit, visited a friend of mine. In searching for something inspirational to read, he looked through her collection of my books and, in my opinion, wisely selected *Open Your Mind to Receive.* This man, through his work, was giving, giving, giving. That book was appropriate for helping him to *receive* as well—to receive his own good. And it's true: we hear so much about giving, but a time comes when we also need to balance things out by opening our minds, hearts, and lives to receiving.

My few short years in San Antonio were "fiesta time," so writing was not a priority for me then, though lecturing on all the books I'd already written certainly was. After such a long period of writing in solitude in Austin, the time had come for Catherine to "come out and play" in San Antonio. Reward time. Divine restoration time.

CHAPTER 14

A Fifty-Year Writing Saga—Part II
From the West Coast

Once I got settled in our first Palm Springs house, a "fixer-upper" with lots of glass, a walled-in back yard, and a view of San Jacinto Mountain looming majestically in the background, I discovered I had an "Associate Editor."

Our ol' dog Taurus had been given to me by my son and named for his—my son's—astrological sign. Taurus was half Basset and half Beagle, so Dr. Bill and I called him "the Bassel." His main claim to fame was that he had reportedly been part of a litter of puppies owned by the family of President Lyndon Johnson. Regardless, I never knew whether he was a Democrat or not.

He slept for hours in my writing studio right behind my steno chair while I wrote at my typewriter. Then, upon being roused from his latest nap, he generally moved quietly through the open sliding glass door to take a walk outside near the pool— often just about the time the afternoon sprinklers were coming on to spray the flowers in the yard. He considered those sprinklers his private shower and, after indulging himself, usually sneaked back in to where I was working, more often than not with wet, dirty paws.

When I finished a manuscript, I customarily placed it on the carpet nearby, to review it page by page and chapter by chapter. But if Taurus had just finished one of his showers, he'd walk all over my manuscript and leave his muddy paw prints everywhere before I could stop him. Since he was such good company while I pounded away day after day at my typewriter, I decided that instead of banishing him, I should put as good a face on his antics as I possibly can.

My solution: I simply sent my manuscripts to my publishers as they were, explaining that the dirty smudges on some of the pages were paw prints of approval from my Associate Editor, my ol' hound dog the Bassel, who kept me company while I wrote. I further explained that I interpreted his paw prints on certain pages or chapters as marks of approval that pointed out his favorite passages.

Did my explanation work? It must have, for the books appeared in print without a murmur from the publisher—at least without a murmur I ever heard—though the paw prints somehow turned invisible, and no sign of them ever showed up on the final printed pages.

HIS OTHER TALENTS

Over and over when friends from out of state visited us in our house in the Old Movie Colony neighborhood, their first question when they returned home and telephoned us was: "How's Taurus?"

That dog could have taught Dale Carnegie a thing or two about winning friends and influencing people. He had his own private fan club.

A friend came to town to edit several manuscripts I had written that needed fine-tuning. As she sat by the pool with my manuscripts in hand, Taurus insisted upon getting in her lap. Nobody could say that dog didn't take his Associate Editor job seriously.

But his uniqueness did not stop there. He was the only dog I ever knew who had his own sports car and chauffeur, and got driven around Palm Springs with the top down while he sniffed the air. He took it all in stride and very nonchalantly, as though it was his due.

He was the only dog I ever knew who sent out Christmas cards and got his own in return. (I put his paw on a stamp pad, pressed it onto a Christmas card to create an imprint, and mailed it for him.) Not only did he get replies, but he also got notes that *analyzed* his paw print, giving good explanations of his personality—and antics.

He was the only dog I ever knew who had his own lawyer, went to court, and won a case against another dog. The judge said he was glad to finally "get" that other dog, who was a big bully and whose owner had been warned about its aggressive behavior before. Yet the dog had arrogantly accosted yet another wannabe friend—amiable Taurus—who was out for a walk. Taurus ended up first at his veterinarian's office, then at the lawyer's office. That big bully had to leave the state under court order.

AN IDENTITY CRISIS?—HARDLY!

Taurus was the only dog I ever knew about whose identity as a dog was actually questioned.

An animal control officer came to our front door one night, identified himself, and said, "I'm here to check on whether you have a dog or not. If so, I'd like to see proof that he's had his proper shots."

My feisty husband considered that visit an invasion of our evening privacy. He was in the process of giving the animal control officer a "non-answer" of sorts when Taurus strolled up and wanted to get in on the action. He began by checking out the officer's shoes and pants, then wagging his tail in friendly fashion.

"So you *do* have a dog," commented the officer.

My husband said, "You mean to tell me you consider that 'critter' a 'dawg'?"

And a verbal battle ensued, with Taurus enjoying all the commotion, especially since it was about him. I never knew the outcome of that confrontation over our "dawg," but I *do* know that no animal control officer ever came near our house again, either night or day, during all the remaining years we lived in that neighborhood. Also, I suspect Taurus knew the Asian philosophy of "treating blame and acclaim the same," since that's what he did. Furthermore, he had no noticeable identity crisis over the incident. If anything, it added to his already healthy self-esteem.

THE TIME HE GOT AWAY

Another unique experience Taurus had that surely added to his self-esteem was the time he managed to run away and could not be found. Some of our staff working in the yard apparently left a gate open, and when no one was looking, Taurus used the opportunity to wander out of his walled-in world. After my husband looked high and low for him for hours, we gave up, though we spent a sleepless night concerned about his being exposed to the cold dark air—wherever he was.

The next morning Dr. Bill telephoned the animal shelter hoping Taurus had been turned in and discovered that he had! During his wandering the day before, he had been picked up by "dognappers," who combed well-to-do neighborhoods looking for beloved pets, then contacted the owners and collected a reward for having "found" the animals.

However, when the dognappers realized that Taurus was a mixed breed and was not even wearing a dog collar with identification, they decided he did not have affluent owners, drove him into downtown Palm Springs, and dropped him in a parking lot.

A lady with several children saw him being removed from the car, which then drove away. She realized he was lost or unwanted, and when her children insisted on taking him home, she finally relented.

There, in his usual nonchalant way, Taurus made himself comfortable and was greatly loved by the houseful of children. After being fed and watered, he relaxed on one of the children's beds for the night and enjoyed all the warmth and comfort of home.

The next morning the mother said to her brood, "This dog is so friendly, he's surely someone's beloved pet. We must take him to the Animal Shelter, just in case. If he hasn't been claimed in a few days, we'll keep him as our own."

And that's where Taurus was when Dr. Bill phoned in.

Whether it was "kidnapping" or "dognapping," Taurus had doubtless enjoyed his getaway into the big, wide world—at least temporarily. I discovered from him that leading a dog's life can have its interesting moments.

MY ASSOCIATE EDITOR—IN SUMMARY

Taurus was with me for almost twenty years, and he has now retired to hound heaven. He is the only dog I ever knew who got fan mail ten years after his death.

When I mentioned him in a magazine article, I think every dog lover who read that article wrote me on his behalf.

As I continue my book-writing in this twenty-first century, I will doubtless also continue to need editing, as I have in the past. But I've made one very serious decision. No more Associate Editors with wet paws.

Why?

Because they're too unforgettable.

THE MILLIONAIRES OF THE BIBLE: THEIR PERSONALITIES

I wrote the first four books in my "Millionaires of the Bible" series in a millionaire neighborhood. There's that Law of Saturation at work again.

In our house in the Old Movie Colony neighborhood, from the tiny study where I worked, I could look out onto the pool, then onto orange trees, palm trees, and bright fuchsia-colored bougainvilleas growing on the side of the house, all with "purple mountain majesties" in the background. It was a far cry and a long way from Mother's kitchen table, where I had begun writing several decades earlier. I had now gotten all my books released from my former publishers and was writing for the long-established West Coast publisher, DeVorss & Co.

THE MILLIONAIRES OF GENESIS
Their Prosperity Secrets for You

Giving birth to a book about the men of Genesis was like giving birth to children. They, with their very different personalities, all came alive in my consciousness and demanded their fair share of attention as I did research about and lecture work on them prior to writing the book.

As father of the Hebrew people, Abraham was much the wealthy aristocrat. However, his son Isaac was so quiet and peaceful that I almost overlooked his importance . . . until I read how he had increased his wealth "a hundredfold" in just one short year. That got my attention.

Jacob, the son of Isaac and definitely a problem child, has been described as "the naughty boy of the Old Testament." But I think of him more as being, in his own way, simply rowdy and demanding. I took up for him in *The Prosperity Secrets of the Ages* as well as in *The Millionaires of Genesis.* He wanted three chapters in the latter book, and I finally gave him two—while everybody else got just one. He neglected to appreciate my generosity and, for ten years, kept bugging me to give him that other chapter. When I finally revised *The Millionaires of Genesis* after that intervening decade, I gave in—and the strong-willed Jacob got his third chapter. Peace at last.

Only the charming billionaire Joseph, who went from pit to palace, gave me no problems. But as some might point out, "When you're a billionaire, what's the problem?"

THE MILLIONAIRE MOSES
His Prosperity Secrets for You

I originally planned to write one book to cover both Moses and Joshua. But Moses would have no part of that. He insisted upon his own book, saying to me in essence, "I am the leader of the Hebrew people, and I won't be crowded out by anybody." So he got his own book, and my further research revealed that he deserved it, as he showed people how to get out of limitation and through their wilderness experiences.

A woman on her way home from work on a New York subway was reading *The Millionaire Moses* when she suddenly realized someone was leaning over her shoulder. Turning around, she discovered that a woman in the seat behind her was reading along with her about the fascinating Moses. They continued reading together for the rest of their subway ride, then the woman who owned the book bade her unexpected reading companion a fond goodbye—after making sure she had enough information to get her own copy of *The Millionaire Moses.*

THE MILLIONAIRE JOSHUA
His Prosperity Secrets for You

I wondered if I would have enough material for a book on Joshua, since I originally planned only to give him two chapters in the Moses book. But when I started doing my research, Joshua seemed to be such a "happy warrior" that I wanted to be certain I gave him the space he so obviously deserved.

At first, when I read in the Bible about his daring exploits, I wondered how I could write about his warrior ways. But he insisted pleasantly on my telling his story. After I did my research and interpretation, it turned out to be quite a tale, and people have loved Joshua ever since. He showed them how to get into their own Promised Land.

I had a Palm Springs florist who loved my books. Every time a new one came out, he sent me roses, often the color of the book cover. When he got the Joshua book, he liked it so much that he just kept sending me bright orange "tea roses"—small, elegant, and all bunched together in beautiful, round, low vases. The effect was spectacular. But so was Joshua, as the first Commanding General of the Hebrews. He would have expected nothing less on his behalf.

THE MILLIONAIRE FROM NAZARETH
His Prosperity Secrets for You

This was a surprise book. Although I had kept the material in my files for twenty years after developing it (having first researched and lectured on the subject in Birmingham), when I finally got around to writing it in Palm Springs, I couldn't *stop* writing. That book just went on and on.

I realized that a whole series of prosperity books based on the four Gospels was possible. So I finally just tried to compress Jesus' basic experiences into that single presentation, hoping I could get back to more volumes on the subject later. Meanwhile, as I wrote it, the size of the book just kept multiplying on me like the loaves and fishes, with plenty left over. And my readers have had similar experiences in multiplying their own abundance.

One reader said, "You are the first minister I have known who emphasized the prosperity teachings of the Bible. What a relief that I no longer have to say, 'I am poor, but I'm a good Christian.' Now I realize that Jesus was not poor, and neither should we be."

THOSE MILLIONAIRES
ANOTHER LOOK

Della Reese, who has long been known by popular music fans as a gifted and successful singer, started a church a number of years ago. I learned about it through an article in a Los Angeles newspaper, which also stated that she was teaching from my "Millionaires of the Bible" series. The celebrated actress/singer, of course, went on to achieve even greater fame as a result of her starring role in the television series *Touched by an Angel*.

Later, I met her in person at an event where we were both speaking. She hugged me so hard that I realized I had not merely been "touched by an angel," but I had, and perhaps more accurately stated, been *squeezed* by an angel. Interesting . . . that the millionaires of the Bible had even made it to Hollywood—big time!

INNER EXPANSION BRINGS OUTER RESULTS

For many years I had been affirming a paraphrase of Psalm 122: "LET THERE BE PEACE WITHIN MY WALLS AND PROSPERITY WITHIN MY PALACES." Although a gradual growth of prosperity had occurred in my own life, the full outpicturing of that paraphrase finally came about when my husband and I found and moved into the old, walled-in estate (the one reportedly first owned by silent-screen star and comic Harold Lloyd) in the historic Las Palmas neighborhood of Palm Springs—another millionaire-celebrity neighborhood.

When I first began using that paraphrase of Psalm 122, I was living in an apartment with no apparent hope of ever having my own home, and a walled-in estate would have seemed out of the question. Nevertheless, I strongly felt I should declare those words often.

At about the same time, I offered that statement—"LET THERE BE PEACE WITHIN MY WALLS AND PROSPERITY WITHIN MY PALACES"—to a friend. He scoffingly asked, "How could that ever happen?" And he refused to use those prosperous words.

Years later, when he passed on, he was still living in a rented apartment. To be sure, living in an apartment is perfectly suited to many people, but in his case I often wonder what might have happened had he dared to join me in using that prosperous paraphrase of the Psalmist.

In my newly acquired guest-house writing studio in that walled-in compound, I worked for twenty years. Along with moving ahead steadily on many other projects, I updated *The Secret of Unlimited Prosperity* and wrote *Dare to Prosper!* and *The Prospering Power of Prayer.* Those little books were and still are especially appropriate as gifts to people who would like—or could use—an introduction to prosperous thinking. Recipients often graduate to other Ponder books thereafter.

One reader noted that she gives away food baskets every holiday, and that she always includes one of those small books. She said, "I believe in feeding the inner person as well."

In an unrelated instance, a homeless man received *Dare to Prosper!* as a gift. He hadn't worked in months, but vowed after reading that book to tithe a tenth of everything he received from any work he got. The very next morning, he found a day-long job. From the $10 he earned, he took a $1 tithe to the nearest church, which was where he had been given that book.

He started attending classes and services, and soon had permanent work, from which he also shared a tenth of what he was paid. A friend, also homeless, saw what happened and asked his secret, whereupon the man showed him his copy of *Dare to Prosper!* The second man began reading the book and immediately got work. His first tithe was $80 from the $800 he soon made—income that seemed like a fortune to him. The two friends kept on attending that church together, as they continued to work, tithe, and prosper.

THAT GOLDEN SUNBURST

My readers have sometimes asked the meaning of the golden sunburst on the covers of my books. One commented: "When I see that gold symbol in a bookstore, I know a Ponder book is involved and I always check it out." Another reader said that's how she *finds* my books—by looking for that sunburst.

The symbol was not an original idea with me. It came from one of my publishers, the late Arthur Peattie of DeVorss & Co., who suggested that we use it on all my books for its beauty and as a symbol of distinction. His suggestion proved to become a popular one.

Here is its meaning, which ties in perfectly with the Wholeness I write about in all of my books: *In ancient times people of note often bore "seals" on their possessions as indications of their success and prominence. The golden sunburst found on the Ponder books is such a seal—one of enlightenment and abundance. Its fifteen points symbolize the breaking up of hard conditions and the expansion that enlightenment can bring—into one's royal heritage of increased health, wealth, and happiness.*

NO END IN SIGHT

Good news: my half-century writing saga continues happily into the new century, with no end in sight!

CHAPTER 15

The Saga Changes To Act Three

After Dr. Bill was gone, I continued to work—while I lived in and enjoyed my Spanish-style home. But by the time the new millennium arrived, I was getting that feeling of divine discontent again, and I sensed the time had come to move on, to release memories of the past that were connected with "the hacienda."

MILLENNIUM TIME

My son, who had relocated to the desert in order to be nearby if and when I needed help, spent time looking for a different living arrangement for me. He found it in another desirable neighborhood, on property that was once occupied by a well-known fast-food magnate. It was to become "Catherine's Millennium Casa."

This comfortable home was a far cry from the closet-size room I occupied as a Government Girl during World War II, or the one room my son and I had to share in my first ministry. It surely was an answer to my prayer so many years ago for my own home, when I had been divinely advised to ". . . seek ye first the kingdom of God, and His righteousness; and all these things shall be added unto you." (Matthew 6:33)

After years of strenuous activity, including the "Have Books, Will Travel" lecture circuit, I anticipated the opportunity to work quietly and enjoy life more fully, and I felt this was the perfect place to do so. Backed up against a mountain, it would be a setting appropriate for my writing the numerous books I planned for the twenty-first century. It would also be an ideal location in which to continue the creative work I had done with my global ministry since 1973—work that was implemented both by me and by my Palm Desert staff.

Now, in Act Three of my life, I no longer work every day around the clock. Instead, on the days I plan to be in my office, I arise at 5 A.M. (having discovered that God is an early riser and that He likes company), enjoy a cup of coffee, have my devotional time, and plan out my staff's tasks for the day. By 7-7:30 A.M., I am at my desk, where I work until early afternoon, while my mental and physical energies are still high. Afterward, I deal with other matters, but in a more relaxed, informal way.

AMONG LIFE'S GREATEST PLEASURES

At a convention recently, after the keynote speech I'd just given, an audience member asked, "What's been your greatest pleasure in the last ten years?"

"Growing older in peace and harmony," I responded.

I acknowledged to the questioner that I was now in Act Three of my life. In the theater, that's when the various themes from the first two acts of a play begin coming together in a satisfying way. "I welcome this period," I said, "along with its particular fringe benefits—less strain and more opportunities to experience the ordinary blessings of life that most people take for granted, but which for many years, I had neither the time nor the money to enjoy."

I observed that after years of other experiences, I was looking forward to returning to my book-writing. "It's great to finally have family and adequate staff helping with the overall responsibilities, and to experience all I've not been able to enjoy, especially in the recent past."

I concluded, "Do not be afraid of Act Three. It can be very rewarding." My audience applauded in approval.

Later, a newspaper reporter who was at that convention wrote about my presentation, describing me in her column as "wearing designer's duds, and chic beyond her years."

Another great rumor.

(Among the additional "what's the greatest" questions I've heard from time to time is this: "After fifty years of creative work in the inspirational field, what do you feel is the greatest theological question of all time?" My response: "Simple. 'How much can I get away with and still go to heaven?'")

ACT THREE CONTINUES

During Act Three, I've enjoyed having more time for contact with longtime friends who have not gone on to the next plane of life. Those who have gone on include my beloved Ponder sister-in-law and also the treasured prayer partner I had for forty years. The list increases in length as the years pass.

I also give special attention to making new friends. I use affirmations that have brought and continue to bring congenial new people into my life: "NEW, SINCERE FRIENDS AND LOVED ONES NOW ENTER MY LIFE, SHOWERING ME WITH THEIR GOODNESS, AND I SHOWERING THEM WITH MY GOODNESS." Also, "THE WORLD IS FULL OF CHARMING PEOPLE WHO NOW LOVINGLY HELP ME IN EVERY WAY, AND I LOVINGLY HELP THEM IN EVERY WAY."

COMPARING OUR FORTY YEARS OF PROGRESS

Miriam, a friend of long-standing, visited me over a recent holiday season. She stayed in my guest house, and we spent many pleasant hours by the fire comparing notes of all we had experienced since we were "sweet young things" together during my Birmingham ministry, more than forty years earlier. What delighted me was the way she had, during the intervening decades, demonstrated the power of inspirational ideas whenever others felt that certain things "couldn't be done."

When I first met her, she was a divorced mother caring for three small children and developing her own business (in an era before that lifestyle was considered acceptable for women). Her children used to play with my son.

In my first ministry, she'd always had a way of sensing when day-to-day circumstances became too much for me to cope with, and she'd call me at church, insisting that we go out for lunch. At first, we had to pool our scanty resources to determine where we could afford to go. But regardless of where we went, we got all dressed up, including hat and gloves.

Knowing about the Law of Saturation, we then proceeded to go to the very best restaurant we could get in, if only for a bowl of soup. We always felt better after those "luncheons," following which we carried on with our professional and family responsibilities.

Knowing her circumstances, the people at the church shook their heads and sadly said, "Too bad about Miriam. She's so attractive and charming, but with all those children, what man could afford to marry her?" Thank goodness, that's not the way *she* was thinking.

The same year I left for Texas and married Kelly Ponder, she went north. There she met and married the heir to an "old money" fortune. She and her new husband had a child of their own, and her husband helped her raise all four of the children. Although he is now deceased, she continues to enjoy the lifestyle and status he provided for her—which includes children and grandchildren.

All those years ago, everyone at the church had been amused when she bought—and constantly wore—a $200 gold suit (a 1950's price). That outfit, which she called her "gold-dust suit," made her look and feel like a million dollars. And, indeed, it helped her demonstrate just that—and more.

Her daughter used to be a restless young child during my Sunday services, often getting more attention than my talk as she moved from one person's lap to another. According to her letters to me and her mother's proud reports, she is now a businesswoman who feels that what she heard as a child at church helped her become a successful professional—conducting prosperity classes and counseling sessions. Yet when she was a little girl in church, I thought she wasn't listening!

FAMILY RECONNECTIONS AND COMMENTS

For the first time since childhood, I have enjoyed regular contact with my sister (a retired schoolteacher) and her husband of fifty years, as well as my brother (who is retired from the United States Air Force) and his wife of more than forty years. Until we recently compared notes, I did not realize that my brother had participated in both the Korean conflict and, later, the Vietnam war—so busy and far apart had we been for several decades.

On our infrequent trips back and forth to visit each other—either they came to the West Coast or I went to the East Coast—they gently suggested that I return to my roots, near them. But they know how much I love the West, with its maverick ways. And they tend to understand my fascination with my tropical surroundings. Nevertheless, whether we're together or not, my sister and I will both have the same outlook about the future. As she once told me, "When the time comes, Sis, we're going to become a couple of 'cool old ladies.'"

Another travel-related discussion with a family member—my son Richard—brought a comment about the past. When I told him I was writing this memoir, he said, "I hope you'll tell your readers that when I was young, you took me everywhere with you." Then he added, "But also be sure to tell them that I always managed to find my way home anyway."

AMONG LIFE'S GREATEST SURPRISES

Although I have received various forms of recognition for my prosperity writings since 1959, the 1990s and the twenty-first century have brought a real surprise, with many public awards, accolades, and tokens of appreciation being bestowed upon me from near and far.[23] The entire universe seemed to have discovered me long ago, but during the 1990s and into this present era, it appears suddenly to have wanted to make sure I am aware of the fact!

---

23. A partial list: Prosperity Teacher of the Century; 2000 Outstanding Writers of the 20th Century; Doctor William H.D. Hornaday Humanitarian Award; Doctor Joseph Murphy Humanitarian Award; Goodwill Ambassador to the World Award; Light of God Expressing Award; World's Who's Who Hall of Fame; 500 Founders of the 21st Century.

Indeed, my readership has been growing for half a century. In this country alone, my books have reached from Broadway to Hollywood. A Catholic priest known as "the Bishop of Broadway" shared my books with many on the great white way as part of his counseling ministry. A Hollywood director on his way to an isolated area to shoot a picture grabbed one of my books that had been given to him. Since there was nothing for his crew and actors to do at night, he offered to start a prosperity study group based on material from my book. Eight people began attending. Soon that study group had grown to eighty. It kept them busy and happy throughout that picture-making experience and beyond.

On the Nashville scene, some of the biggest names in country music have spread my books among their peers, near and far. Dolly Parton, in her autobiography,[24] mentioned that some of my books have been of help to her.

Internationally, my books have had a varied though always positive impact. A twelve-year-old girl wrote from Ireland, "Why do I always 'see' green around *The Dynamic Laws of Prosperity* when I am studying it?"

I replied, "Probably because that color symbolizes both prosperity and growth, as in 'green but growing.'"

A young Communist in Asia found one of my prosperity books at the library. He wrote, "I became a Communist in order to prosper, but it didn't work. Your book did. I'll never be a Communist again."

In parts of the world where political factions would have prohibited my writings from entering the country through the usual channels, they got there anyway! An

---

24. *Dolly: My Life and Other Unfinished Business*, by Dolly Parton (1994, HarperCollins, New York), p. 305.

Ambassador, using his diplomatic immunity, took my books into some of those countries via his diplomatic pouch and shared them with people he felt would be interested and find them beneficial. I never dreamed I'd ever have my own private diplomatic courier!

MULTIFACETED RESULTS

The field of religion has been similarly affected. A world-famous evangelist whose name had long been familiar to me and to the world startled me when he wrote that he had used the messages in my books in his evangelistic work for years. A rabbi who was fascinated with my "Millionaires of the Old Testament" books based a study group on them. Everyone prospered—so greatly that he finally disbanded the group because everyone's need had been met!

When people write me and say they are not near a church or study group that teaches the ideas expressed in my books, I always suggest they start their own group. The result is that people of all ages, in all walks of life, from all belief systems—and also from none— quietly meet and study my books around the world. Some meet before work, others at lunchtime, others after work, and still others at night or on weekends.

One reader, a businessman in Nigeria, West Africa, conducted a study group every night of the year after work for twenty years, until his death. His students continue to write me of their rewarding experiences.

Another reader, from Ghana, West Africa, asked if he might name the twenty churches he headed "The Catherine Ponder Memorial Churches."

I replied, "Yes, with one exception. Please leave out that word 'Memorial,' because I'm not dead yet. And God isn't finished with me."

I now hear from the children and grandchildren of my original readers. My staff's records reflect that the Ponder books have reached into all fifty of the United States and many dozens of countries. My files are bulging with innumerable reports of good news on every level of life, and from all points on the globe.

AMONG THE MOST GRATIFYING RESULTS

One of the most gratifying results of a half-century of writing and lecturing about prosperity and related subjects is that writers and lecturers from later generations, up to and including the present one, are now doing the same thing. When I began my work decades ago, I felt like a voice in the wilderness. Indeed, I *was* a voice in the wilderness. For many years I was the only woman author with a nationwide audience who was writing and lecturing on prosperity. Even the number of men who were doing so was relatively small, consisting principally of Dr. Norman Vincent Peale, Dr. Maxwell Maltz, business tycoon W. Clement Stone, and longtime success-writer Napoleon Hill.

And now, I rejoice in all the books, seminars, workshops, courses, and meetings that are available to the public on these subjects, by a variety of authors and speakers in various secular and nonsecular settings. The twenty-first century is truly on its way to the greater abundance we all deserve!

A MIXED MESSAGE

Anything I write about the last fifty years of my life can only touch the surface of all that has happened— the wonderful and sometimes not-so-wonderful people who have come and gone, and the countless interesting experiences that have also come and gone (they are too numerous to recite here, though many are found in my other books).

Gandhi is well-known for his statement, "Your life is your message." If mine seems a mixed message, that *is* life: a mixture of blessings, challenges, teaching, and learning. My brother may well have summed up my long-term experience when he said, "Catherine, you have proved that life's limitations do not have to be terminal."

After a convention lecture, I was asked the secret of my success, and I cited my answer to a lady who once wrote me and asked, "I have read *all* your books *all* the way through. *Now* what do I do?"

The answer I sent back to her was simple. "Practice, dear. Practice."

THE GREATEST LOVE STORY OF ALL

But the greatest love story of all is about my finally having found that "special and different" something I always knew I was supposed to do in life—and that I have been busy doing ever since, in one form or another.

And all of that time, my different drummer has still been busy playing my own special tune, so "the beat goes on."

A PROSPERITY LOVE STORY IN SUMMARY

I trust you have become aware through these pages of the prosperity love story this book contains:

Prosperity

1) Putting God first through sharing and tithing;

2) Affirming, declaring, and meditating upon prosperity prayer-statements;

3) Picturing greater good on prayer maps or wheels of fortune;

4) Practicing forgiveness and release, "giving up" that which is no longer for your highest good, whether in inner or outer ways;

5) Planning a course to success, then working the plan by staying focused on it, no matter what;

6) And finally, giving thanks for life's blessings and setting aside daily devotional periods for reading selections from your favorite inspirational book, the thought-for-the-day in *Daily Word* or *Science of Mind* magazine, or a passage from the Bible or from whatever belief system appeals to you.

Love

The great love stories of my life have been about:

1) The inspirational teaching I found just when I needed it most and have shared worldwide;

2) The people who touched me deeply.

Conclusion

YOUR IMPORTANCE

"One person can make a difference and every person should try."

I tried. Oh, how I have tried! And as you do, too, your inner and outer efforts can lead you and countless others first to enlightenment and then to enrichment—on whatever levels of life are most appropriate, on whatever levels you feel a need.

As a friend of mine has often said, "Life . . . what a trip!" You can draw your own conclusions concerning my varied life experiences. As for your own, these declarations can help you to claim your own private love story, in both universal and personal ways:

For the past, declare often, "I TAKE THE GOOD FROM EACH EXPERIENCE. I LET THE REST GO."

For now and future, declare, "DIVINE LOVE, EXPRESSING THROUGH ME, NOW DRAWS TO ME ALL THAT IS NEEDED TO MAKE ME HAPPY AND TO MAKE MY LIFE COMPLETE."

Happy landing!

Catherine Ponder
P. O. Box 1536
Palm Desert, CA 92261
USA

Snapshots and Photographs

Revolution and Historiography

Government Girl WWII
Washington, D.C.

Author & son
Birmingham, Alabama

Catherine & Kelly Ponder
Austin, Texas

Lecture time
San Antonio & elsewhere

Autographing time
U.S. & abroad

Award time
U.S. & abroad

Author & son, 21st Century
Palm Springs, California, and elsewhere

Thank You!

for selecting this book from DeVorss Publications. If you would like to receive a complete catalog of our specialized selection of current and classic Metaphysical, Spiritual, Inspirational, Self-Help, and New Thought books, please visit our website or give us a call and ask for your free copy.

DeVorss Publications
devorss.com • 800-843-5743